—40—
Assemblies
for Infants

40 Assemblies for Infants

Rachel Boxer and Paul Gateshill

Heinemann Educational Publishers
Halley Court, Jordan Hill, Oxford OX2 8EJ
a division of Reed Educational & Professional Publishing Ltd

OXFORD FLORENCE PRAGUE MADRID ATHENS
MELBOURNE AUCKLAND KUALA LUMPUR SINGAPORE TOKYO
IBADAN NAIROBI KAMPALA JOHANNESBURG GABORONE
PORTSMOUTH NH (USA) CHICAGO MEXICO CITY SAO PAULO

Heinemann is a registered trademark of Reed Educational & Professional
Publishing Ltd

00 99 98

10 9 8 7 6 5 4 3 2 1

British Library Cataloguing in Publication Data

A catalogue record for this book is available from the British Library

ISBN 0 435 30236 1

Designed by Artistix

Cover design by Threefold Design

Typeset by TechType

Printed and bound in Great Britain by The Bath Press, Bath

Acknowledgements

The publishers would like to thank Gareth Boden for permission to
reproduce the cover photograph.

The publishers have made every effort to trace copyright holders. However,
if any material has been incorrectly acknowledged, we would be pleased to
correct this at the earliest opportunity.

Contents

Our world

Stories from religions

Effective strategies

Two-year rolling programme

Resources and useful addresses

Preface

This book is the result of cries for help from those fraught teachers and head teachers who are struggling with the legal requirement to provide daily collective worship for four to seven-year-olds. Many books purporting to cater for infants are, in reality, aimed more at Key Stage 2 pupils and tend to reinforce frustration. This book, however, starts off from the authors' experience that:

- many four-year-olds find it difficult even to face the right way!
- four to seven-year-olds have a limited concentration span
- infants are mysterious, unfathomable creatures – adults may think we know what is going on inside their little heads but ...

We were also aware that when published assembly materials *do* succeed in catering for Key Stage 1 pupils, they are often reluctant to deal with explicit religious ideas and beliefs, and it is difficult to see how they can be described as meeting the legal requirements of Collective Worship. This book therefore attempts to achieve a balance between a child-centred approach and the requirements of the 1988 Education Act that 'collective worship should be wholly or mainly of a broadly Christian character'.

We spent a long time thinking of a title. The best one seemed to be 'Lots and lots of little children in a very small hall' but it wouldn't fit snugly on the cover. Therefore we eventually went for the less imaginative, but perhaps more informative, *40 Assemblies for Infants*.

Most of the assemblies in this book have been tried and tested with real, live four-to-seven-year-olds. Obviously this does not mean that they can be just taken off the shelf as an instant recipe for success but, hopefully, the knowledge that someone out there has made them work might give you some reason for confidence! We wish you well.

Rachel Boxer and Paul Gateshill

About the authors

Rachel Boxer is currently teaching five-to-six-year-olds at Beaufort Primary School, Woking, Surrey. She is the Co-ordinator for Religious Education, Collective Worship and Assessment.

Paul Gateshill is County Consultant for Personal, Social and Religious Education in Surrey. Prior to this, he was Professional Officer for RE with the School Curriculum and Assessment Authority.

Dedication

This book is dedicated to all you enthusiastic, hard-working, paper-weary, heroic teachers for whom assemblies are often the last straw. May this book lighten your load and brighten your day!

Acknowledgements

The authors would like to thank:

- Blue Class at Beaufort Primary School (Autumn '96 – Summer '97)
- all the staff at Beaufort Primary, especially those who have said encouraging things about many of the assemblies in this book
- Anna Brodrick for allowing us to include her ideas in 'Just around the corner'
- Peter Jackson for the ideas behind 'Building walls', 'Co-operation', 'Watch what you say' and 'The hardest word'
- Allan Wells for 'We are all special'
- Ann Lovelace for her inspiring workshops on assemblies
- Rachel Pottinger for her help with ideas for music.

Introduction

We have deliberately used the terms 'assembly' and 'collective worship' throughout this book in a rather loose and interchangeable way. Although 'collective worship' is the legal term, we feel that the word 'assembly' is much more apt for Key Stage 1. Some people prefer to use the term 'assembly' for the notice-giving element of the school gathering and 'collective worship' for the moment of reflection or 'worship'. We feel that although this is a useful distinction for planning, it is more apt as a description for secondary schools than for the primary sector.

This is not the place to debate the nature of collective worship within schools. This has been well-discussed in a variety of professional and commercial publications. We have, however, ensured that the assemblies outlined here meet legal requirements and are 'wholly or mainly of a broadly Christian character' (Education Act 1988). However, in line with the guidance from the DfEE (Circular 1/94), this does not preclude schools from celebrating festivals, beliefs and values from other faiths and secular society. We have, therefore, written this book based on our own conviction that collective worship provides Key Stage 1 pupils with opportunities to:

- celebrate being part of a school community
- explore areas which directly concern them
- broaden their awareness of themselves, others and the world in which they live
- become reflective, deep-thinking individuals in a frenetic and complex society
- explore their own beliefs and values, alongside the beliefs and values of others
- deepen understanding of their own culture and recognize that cultural diversity is enriching rather than threatening.

In short, collective worship should be seen as an excellent opportunity for promoting the spiritual, moral, social and cultural development of pupils.

Assembly format

For ease of use, the assemblies have been organized following a common format. Each assembly uses a selection of the following headings:

Introduction	designed to give an overall flavour of the assembly, based on the experience of trying it out with Key Stage 1 pupils
Resources	based on what most schools would easily have available
Timing	realistic – and the length can be adjusted by adapting the assemblies
Preparation	realistic and, hopefully, not too daunting: many of the ideas could be prepared with your own class
The Assembly	step-by-step for the uninitiated, but not, we hope, too patronizing for the initiated
Reflection	examples intended to encourage children to be still and reflective for a short while, and may even help promote pupils' spiritual, moral, social and cultural development
Prayer	an example of a prayer which should meet legal requirements, but which would also be accessible to Muslim, Jewish, Hindu and Sikh pupils
Suggestions for music	some suggestions which are readily available.

Prayers and/or reflections?

The whole issue of **prayer** in collective worship is a minefield and needs some comment here. Many head teachers and others involved in taking assemblies feel uncomfortable about leading prayers with infants. This might be due to their own lack of commitment to a faith, or perhaps to their discomfort about possibly indoctrinating pupils into a particular set of beliefs. We have therefore included examples of prose to aid reflection, and some possible prayers.

The **reflections** are designed with two purposes. They help to still the children and encourage them to think deeply, perhaps also preparing the ground for the prayer. They could also be used by those who feel unable to lead a prayer, for whatever reason.

The prayers have been formulated so that they are not exclusively Christian, but are acceptable to most faiths. For example, although Christians may refer to God as Father, this is not a concept that would be easily embraced by Muslims, so in this book we have adopted the less emotive form of address, 'Dear God'. These prayers can also be easily adapted and, with a little editing, can be used to end the reflection.

Some teachers use phrases such as 'Let us sit quietly and think or pray for a while about what we have just heard ...' or 'I am going to put my thoughts into a prayer and you can join in with me, if you like, by saying "Amen" at the end'. Simple phrases like these can make the whole act of collective worship a unifying rather than a divisive experience.

Effective assemblies

Not every assembly needs to be dynamic and dripping with pupil participation. This is neither realistic, nor healthy for the hard-pressed Key Stage 1 teacher. Most of the assemblies in this book are in the region of 15–20 minutes long. Assemblies can also be just as effective if they are only of 5–10 minutes duration.

Why are we here?

Introduction

Is this assembly, the first of a new academic year, the one that most teachers in your school would prefer to avoid? It's probably the hardest assembly to present because everything in school is different: new teachers for the children, new classes for us. It is hard to pitch the assembly at the right level. So, if you've drawn the short straw, here's an assembly for you! It needs very little preparation, and aims to keep children involved.

Resources

- a large bag to be used as a 'feelie' bag. (A box could be used, but a bag is better, since objects can remain hidden from the children.)
- a calendar or diary
- a balloon (deflated)
- some card, which needs to be fairly thick to prevent it from getting bent in the bag
- a story book – a Bible could be used to introduce the idea of stories that are special to Christians
- *Five Minutes Peace* by Jill Murphy (if you have access to a copy).

Timing

10–15 minutes

Preparation

On the card, draw and cut out a circle, a speech bubble and a 'think' bubble. Draw a happy face on one side of the card circle, and a sad face on the other side. In the speech bubble, write 'Dear God, ...'. Place these, along with the other objects, into the 'feelie' bag.

These objects will help the children to understand why they go to assembly, and provide you with helpful prompts.

The Assembly

(Welcome the children back to school and to the first assembly of the year. Explain to the children that you want to think for just a few minutes about why we come into the hall to have an assembly. Then tell them that you are going to need some very good helpers. Invite one child at a time to come to the front and feel in your 'feelie' bag. As an object is brought out, the child should return to their place, then you can talk briefly about it, using the following comments as guidelines.)

(The calendar or diary) This is a calendar, which people write on to help them to remember important days. The calendar reminds us that, in our assemblies, we can think about days and times which are important and special to each of us.

(The balloon) When do you have balloons? *(Hopefully, someone will suggest 'at a party'.)* The balloon reminds us that in our assemblies, we can celebrate happy times together.

(The happy/sad face) Look at both sides. What do you see? The happy and sad faces are to remind us that, in our assemblies, we can think about feelings – ours and other people's.

(The think bubble) Do you know what this is? This think bubble reminds us that in our assemblies we can think about things that are important to us.

(The speech bubble) Can anyone read what is written in the speech bubble? The speech bubble reminds us that our assemblies can be times when we talk to God, or pray, which is what talking to God is called. Our prayers often start 'Dear God, ...'.

(The special story book) This Bible is to remind us that, in our assemblies, we can listen to special stories about what people believe.

(Five Minutes Peace) Does anyone know this story? It's all about Mrs Large, an elephant, who is desperate to find a place where she can have some peace and quiet. All of us need peace and quiet sometimes, for all sorts of reasons. This story reminds us that our assemblies are times when we can share some peace and quiet, away from our busy classrooms.

(The children may expect you to read the story to them. If they do, you could save it for the end, or promise that you will read it at story time, or in another assembly.)

Reflection

Let us just sit quietly for a moment and think about how good it is for us to have time to be together – times to think and talk, to listen and learn.

May our assemblies this year be times that are really special for each one of us.

(Pause for a few moments, then continue only if you are going to use the prayer.)

I am going to say a prayer. If you agree with what I say, you can join in with 'Amen' at the end.

Prayer

Dear God,
It is good for us to have time to be together – times to think and talk, to listen and learn. Please make our assemblies this year times that are really special for each one of us.

Amen.

Suggestions for music

'Caribbean Blue' from *Shepherd Moons* by Enya

How to mend a broken heart

Introduction

This is a relatively quick and easy assembly to prepare, and is an effective way of catching pupils' interest. Its aim is to encourage children to think about how their actions can affect other people. It could be used as part of a series of assemblies on the theme of 'Feelings', or as a one-off in response to playground or classroom incidents.

Resources

- a large, red heart-shape cut from paper or card
- Blu-tac
- a board large enough to place the heart onto. (An easel is ideal as the children can see what you are doing.)

Timing

20 minutes – maybe slightly more or less, depending on children's responses.

Preparation

Ask your own class to suggest some things that can hurt people's feelings e.g. breaking a promise, saying hurtful things . These comments will be discussed in the assembly, and children will be given opportunities to suggest the opposite (e.g. keeping a promise, saying kind things).

Choose the best comments from the class to be written on the heart – not too many, or the puzzle becomes too difficult to complete! About six would be ideal.

Cut the paper heart into jigsaw pieces – one for each comment. (It's worth numbering them in pencil on the reverse to help when you do the puzzle.)

Write each comment on a piece of jigsaw puzzle. Use a pen that won't show through on the reverse since the puzzle will be completed with the writing on the back. At this stage, it's worth practising a few times, to get the pieces in the right place.

Use Blu-tac to stick the pieces around the assembly hall before the pupils come in.

The Assembly

Welcome the children and explain that today you have a broken puzzle and are going to need a few helpers, especially children who like doing jigsaws. Tell them that the puzzle is of a heart, and it has been broken because of some sad things that have happened. Say that by the end of the assembly today, you hope to have mended this broken heart.

Ask the children to look around the room, and raise their hand if they can see a piece of jigsaw. Choose children, one at a time, to find a piece close to them, and bring it to you.

Read what is written on the jigsaw piece (or the child can read it if they are able to), then talk about it with the children, relating it to their own experiences where possible. Instead of doing what is written on the puzzle, can they suggest what they should do instead? As each piece is finished with, stick it in position on the board, with the writing on the back. Use the numbers to help you.

Continue, until all the pieces have been discussed, then look at the whole heart.

Finally, explain that it is very easy to hurt people on the inside, and that we all need to try hard to be kind and loving towards others in what we say and do.

Reflection

Let us be still for a moment and think about what we have talked about today. It is so easy to hurt other people's feelings, by what we say to them and what we do to them. Next time we think about saying or doing something hurtful, help us to remember the broken heart puzzle and to be kind and loving instead.

Prayer

Dear God,
It is so easy to hurt other people's feelings, by what we say and what we do. Help us to try to be always kind and loving towards our friends and family, even when we find it hard.

Amen.

Suggestions for music

'Largo' from *Double Concerto in B flat for Oboe, Violin, Strings and Basso Continuo* by Antonio Vivaldi

'Fragile' by Sting

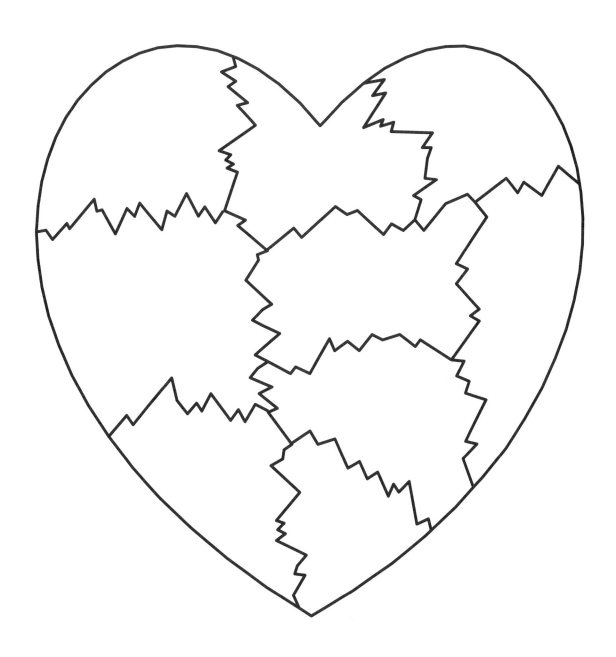

Fun, but not fair!

Introduction

This is a light-hearted introduction to the theme of rules and why we need them. It's based on the well-known game of snakes and ladders, but with a difference. There is little to prepare, especially if you have an overhead projector for the game. Expect a rather more lively assembly than usual, even more so if you make up really unfair rules!

Resources

- an overhead projector (or easel and paper with a large snakes and ladders board)
- the game board photocopied onto a photocopiable OHP acetate and coloured with OHP pens, if desired, or the game drawn on a large sheet of paper, or a commercially-produced board if an OHP is not available
- as many counters as players (two is ideal) and a dice, the larger the better. (Make sure that the counters you choose do not cover a whole square, it makes the rest of the board harder to see.)
- Blu-tac to stick the counters to the board if you're not using the OHP.

Timing

15–20 minutes, depending on how long the game lasts

The Assembly _____

(Welcome the children and explain that today we are going to be thinking about rules. Can anyone tell you what a rule is?

Switch on the OHP or bring out the game and ask if anyone knows what game this is. Ask them if they can tell you the rules.

Choose two children to play – or you could divide the whole hall in half and have the two players as team leaders, to keep everyone involved.

Then explain that we are going to play the game according to your rules, and that there is only one rule – 'I make it up as I go along'. Player 1 throws the dice, and then it's time for you to improvise. Here are some unfair suggestions.

- *count backwards*
- *tell them they have to throw again, for no reason – especially if they are near to a ladder that they think they will be going up!*
- *go down the ladders and up the snakes sometimes*
- *go up the ladders and down the snakes sometimes*
- *tell them they can't go up a particular snake or ladder when they land on it.*

Make the game as long or short as you feel the children can cope with – just change the rules. Have fun!

When somebody has won, wait for the children to settle, then continue.)

Now that game wasn't really fair, was it? Why not? (*Hopefully, a child will suggest that it was because you kept changing the rules as you went along.*) That's right, I made up my own rules. It might have been fun for me, but it certainly wasn't fair on the children playing my game. Just think what would happen if all the games we played had made-up rules. It would never be fair then, would it? Why do you think a game needs rules? (*Wait for suggestions.*) A game needs rules so that everyone plays the game the same way, to make it fair.

Now, our lives are full of rules too – we have some at school. Can you tell me any? (*Wait for suggestions again.*) We have these rules to make our school a fair place for everybody to be in – we don't want our school to be a place filled with rubbish, or where children get hurt because they have been allowed to run in the corridors, do we? (*Change this if you need to, and adapt to your school's rules.*)

Even grown-ups have rules to follow, rules that are decided by important people in our country – such as driving on the left-hand side of the road, stopping at red traffic lights, having to go to work at a certain time, not stealing from people. There are lots and lots of rules in our lives, all of them to keep us safe and make life fair for everybody.

Some people have special books or stories that give them rules to help them live their lives. Christians read the Bible; Muslims read the Qur'an; Jews read the Torah. These people believe that God gave them rules to show them how to live their lives in a better way, for themselves and for others.

Reflection

Let's have a few moments of quiet now to think about what we have heard today.

We have been thinking today about the rules that are part of our lives, rules that make life fair for everyone. As we grow up, may we always try to keep to the rules, wherever we are.

Prayer

Dear God,
We have been thinking about the rules that are part of our lives, and why we need them. It's not always easy to keep to the rules – help us, we pray.

Amen.

Suggestions for music

'Adagietto' from *Symphony no. 5* by Mahler

'Play the game' by Queen

21	22	23	24	25
20	19	18	17	16
11	12	13	14	15
10	9	8	7	6
1	2	3	4	5

Sticky fingers

Introduction

The story of a little boy, who, in my family, was for ever afterwards to be called 'Sticky Fingers', was one of my favourites when I was a child. It was one of many cautionary tales that my grandfather used to tell us – all from memory! It's basically a warning against being greedy, but further meanings can be found if you look carefully.

Resources

- (optional) some real sticky buns – just in case children don't know what a sticky bun looks like (and you can always eat them afterwards).

Timing

15–20 minutes

The Assembly

(Welcome the children and introduce the story.)

Do you have a favourite treat to eat? (*Ask some children – tell them yours, too!*) Well, the little boy in this story had a favourite treat – sticky buns! (*Show the buns if you have them.*) Unfortunately, he wasn't always a very nice little boy, and one day, the sticky buns taught him a very important lesson ...

The story of Sticky Fingers

Once there was a little boy, who was eleven years old and lived with his mum and dad. He had no brothers and sisters, and you might say that he was rather spoilt. He had lots of toys that he loved to play with, but he wasn't very good at sharing. In fact, he was quite selfish, and he soon found that his friends were finding other friends to play with. So he became unhappy and quite lonely.

One day, when he was walking home from school by himself, he stopped to look in the window of the baker's shop, which he passed every day. There, in the window, was his favourite treat – shiny, gooey, sticky buns, 20p each. He rushed in quickly, to make sure that he bought them before anybody else could, and he came out of the baker's shop with two, one in each hand. What a very silly thing to do. He always had cake for tea at home, and his mum would probably be cross with him for spoiling his appetite – but the little boy didn't care.

Just as he turned the corner into his road, he spotted a little girl from his class, with all her younger brothers and sisters. Her family were quite poor, and wouldn't be having cake for tea, like he would. He showed the children his shiny, sticky buns and their faces lit up in excitement. 'I suppose you'd like one of these, wouldn't you?' he said. 'Well, you're not going to get one!' What a selfish and rude little boy!

So he carried on walking until he got home for his tea. Needless to say, he didn't eat very much because he was full of sticky bun. 'Have you been eating on the way home?' his mum asked him. 'Sticky buns,' the little boy replied. 'And did you wash your hands afterwards?' He shook his head. 'Well go and wash them right now!' The little boy went upstairs, but walked straight past the bathroom and into his bedroom – he was in no mood to do as he was told. It was lovely and warm in his room, and he stretched out on his bed, full up and tired. After a while, he went to his toy cupboard and took out his two favourite toys (*Insert two current favourites here.*). He quickly got bored, but when he went to put them down and get something else out, they wouldn't come off his hands – they were stuck fast! Had someone put glue on the buns? Then there'd be glue in his tummy as well!

He ran down the stairs to his mother, yelling, 'Look! Look!' His mother said, 'You didn't wash your hands did you?' and put his hands under the hot water tap. But still the toys were stuck fast. Their next door neighbour suggested rubbing some slippery Vaseline onto his hands to try to make the toys slide off, but it didn't work. Then the little boy's dad came home, and he and the little boy's mum tried to pull the toys off. But no luck.

'We'd better take him to the doctor's – get his coat,' said his dad. But the little boy couldn't even put his coat on because the toys in his hands were too big to go through the sleeves. So they had to put his coat round his shoulders. When they got there, the doctor said, 'I've never seen anything like this before – you'll have to take him to the hospital in the morning. Let's hope they have more luck.' The little boy was nearly in tears by now, and was sorry that he'd ever seen those shiny, sticky buns.

As they were walking home, the little boy spotted the same girl from his class who he'd teased before. She was looking for the pocket money that she'd dropped when she was going to the shops to buy a few sweets for her younger brother's birthday. She'd been searching for a long time, and now she was crying. 'Here,' said the little boy's dad. 'Take this money.' 'Here,' said

Sticky Fingers, 'take my ____ (*Name the two toys.*).' Then, 'Look, Dad! They've come unstuck!' What a relief – he wouldn't have to go to the hospital in the morning after all.

Then, he rolled over on his bed, and woke up!

What can we learn from this story?

The little boy may have only been dreaming, but do you think he'd learnt his lesson? (*Ask some children for their opinions.*) What do you think it was that made the toys come off the little boy's hands?

There are times when each of us is tempted to be greedy, and keep the best for ourselves. There are times when we don't want others to share what we have, just like Sticky Fingers. This may be only a story, but stories can teach us things.

Reflection

Let's have a few moments to be quiet now and think about what we can learn from the story of Sticky Fingers. The story showed us a little boy who was unhappy because he was greedy and selfish. Let's sit still for a moment and think about times when we have not shared ... and times when we have shared ...

Let us always try hard to share and be generous.

Prayer

Dear God,
When we are tempted to be selfish, help us to share.
When we have plenty, help us to be generous.

Amen.

Suggestions for music

'Scherzo' from *The Sorcerer's Apprentice* by Dukas

'Love is something, if you give it away' by Malvina Reynolds (to sing)

'Another day in paradise' by Phil Collins

If at first you don't succeed …

Introduction

This assembly is quick and easy to prepare, and can make use either of your class, or of children in the assembly. The story that accompanies it is a tale of perseverance and could be used on its own for a slightly shorter assembly. Much has been said about the need for children to self-evaluate, and the preparation for this assembly gives them a useful opportunity.

Resources

- an overhead projector (or a large piece of paper clipped to an easel)
- an OHP acetate and black OHP pen.

Timing

15–20 minutes if children are involved

10 minutes if only the story and reflection are used

Preparation

If you are planning to use your class, explain to them that you will be asking for their help, and they will need to think very hard about something they find difficult. You may need to give a few examples, such as tidying up, eating all their lunch, listening carefully, doing as they are told, as well as the more academic skills.

Give them a few moments to think, then get them to tell you what they find difficult, starting their sentences with 'I could try harder to … '. Some children find this hard, so only use children in the assembly who do not mind sharing their weaknesses!

On the OHP acetate or paper, draw some spokes radiating out from a central point, and the start of a spider's web like this:

These will form part of a giant web that you and your class will build up in front of the assembled children. Leave as many blank spokes as there are children saying sentences.

Alternatively, you could use just the children sitting in assembly for suggestions, rather than making a class preparation – it's more risky though!

The Assembly

(Welcome the children and then introduce the story.)

There is a saying that some grown-ups use which goes like this: 'If at first you don't succeed, try, try, try again.' All it means is that when things go wrong, when you feel like giving up, keep on trying until you eventually get it right. It's not always easy to do. Everyone feels like giving up sometimes! We are going to start today's assembly with a very old story about a very small creature – a spider – that helped somebody quite important to keep on going when he felt like giving up.

The story of Robert the Bruce and the spider

In times gone by, our country was not always a peaceful place, and people have often had to fight for the freedom to live in the way they believe is right. Today, our country is made up of Scotland, England, Wales and Northern Ireland, but it has not always been so. About 700 years ago, each part of our country had its own king to rule over the people who lived there.

The king of England wanted, more than anything, to make himself king of Scotland. The king of Scotland at that time was a man called Robert the Bruce, and he was a good and fair king. He gathered a small army and prepared his soldiers for fighting, to keep the English king from taking over.

One night, the English army did a terrible thing. They attacked while the Scottish soldiers were sleeping, and they killed many of Robert the Bruce's men. Robert the Bruce, and those of his soldiers that were left alive, fled to the hills for safety. For some time they lived in caves, hidden from the English soldiers, marching further into Scotland only when it was safe to do so. As time went by, life became more and more difficult, and Robert the Bruce found it harder and harder to keep on going. Everything looked so hopeless – maybe the English would take his country away from him after all.

At the very moment when he was thinking these desperate thoughts, he happened to look at the roof of the cave he was resting in. There, dangling from the ceiling, was a tiny spider. The spider was trying to spin its web, but just as it got near to finishing, a gust of wind would blow on the delicate web, and the web would fall apart. Each time this happened, the little spider would start all over again – even when the web had been destroyed by the wind many times.

As he was watching, Robert the Bruce thought to himself, 'If that little spider can keep on trying to succeed, maybe I should, too.' So, instead of giving up, he decided that he would continue to fight for his country.

There were many more battles that he had to face, but eventually he was victorious. And all because, so the story goes, he watched a little spider trying to spin its web.

Reflection

Let us sit still for a few moments and think about things that we find hard to do.

The spider taught Robert the Bruce to try, try and try again, even when things looked really hopeless. There will be many times in our lives when things are difficult, and we feel like giving up. When this happens to us, may we be the sort of people who, like the spider, will try, try, try again.

(At this point, either go on to the prayer, or explain that in your class you have been thinking about things that you find difficult, and that some children are going to tell you about them.

Explain that we are going to try to build up this broken spider's web as we say what we are going to try harder at.

As they say their sentence, either let them draw a section of web – show them how beforehand – or you draw the web. The idea is that the web is completed as the last child says their sentence.)

Prayer

Dear God,
There are things in our lives which we find hard.
When we feel like giving up, remind us of the little spider
who tried, tried and tried again.

Amen.

Suggestions for music

'Give a little whistle' – Jiminy Cricket's song from Disney's *Pinocchio*

Building walls

Introduction

This assembly needs little preparation, and is a clear illustration of the effect that our words and actions can have on someone else.

Resources

- some bricks of different colours
- a table to build a wall on
- a rolled-up pair of socks – preferably long socks, to make quite a big ball
- an overhead projector, OHP acetate and OHP pens (or the usual easel and paper if the OHP is not an option).

Timing

15–20 minutes

Preparation

Draw a brick wall onto OHP acetate – the bricks should be quite large, so that you can write inside them.

Before the assembly starts, build a wall on the table, several rows high, using the bricks. The rolled-up socks will be thrown at the wall, to try to knock it down. Rolled-up socks are better than a soft ball because they are heavier, and you want the brick wall to be knocked down quite easily – the point will be lost otherwise. It would be advisable for you to practise knocking the wall down beforehand – you may need to find an alternative ball.

The Assembly

(Welcome the children and explain that in today's assembly, we are going to be thinking about feelings.

Show them your brick wall and ask for a volunteer who thinks they will be able to knock the wall down really easily. Tell the volunteer to look at the wall very carefully before they knock it down. The act of knocking down the wall will probably generate a spontaneous round of applause!

Then tell the volunteer that they must build the wall up again – so that it looks exactly like it did before it was knocked down. The volunteer should find this quite difficult, but they don't have to complete the task – just let them keep going long enough for all the children to realize it's much easier to knock down a wall than it is to build it up again. Let them sit down, then continue.)

Which do you think was easier – knocking the wall down, or building it up again exactly the same as it had been? I think it was much easier to knock all the bricks over – when you were building the wall up, you had to try to remember where each brick went. I'm not sure I could manage it any better than you did.

Now the wall is very like our feelings – it is quite easy to hurt someone's feelings by the things that we say, just like it was quite easy to knock down the brick wall. Some things that people say to us can hurt us inside, make us feel sad – I'm sure all of you have been upset by something that someone has said to you.

Sometimes the things we say to other people can either knock down their feelings inside, or build them up to be like a strong wall. Think for a few moments of good things that you could say to your friends – things that will make them feel strong and happy inside. *(Be prepared to give a few examples if necessary – such as 'You tried really hard to build that wall up,' or 'I'd like to play your game this playtime.' As children give suggestions, write each one on a new brick in the wall on the OHP, starting from the bottom and working upwards.)*

Reflection

Let us just take a few moments to look at the wall that the children have built up, and think about how we can make people happy and strong inside.

Prayer

Dear God,
All of us have feelings, and we know how much it hurts inside when someone upsets us. Help us to remember that what we say and what we do can knock people's feelings down, or build them up. Help us to try always to say good things to others.

Amen.

Suggestions for music

'Summer: Adagio' from *The Four Seasons* by Antonio Vivaldi

'I'd like to teach the world to sing' by Backer, Davis, Cook and Greenaway

Co-operation

Introduction

This assembly looks quite long, but that's because of the repetitious nature of the story! It puts a different slant on a story which the children will probably know well. Little preparation is needed.

Resources

- eight large card labels, each with a string attached for hanging round a child's neck
- eight children (or you could use adults if you fancy a change, and they are willing!)
- a few props – a hat for the old man, scarf for the old woman etc.

Timing

20 minutes

Preparation

Take each card label and write the name of one of the characters on one side, and a letter on the other side, as follows:

Old man – T	Old woman – O
Little boy – G	Little girl – E
Dog – T	Cat – H
Duck – E	Mouse – R

Attach string to each label so that it can be hung round its volunteer's neck.

The Assembly

Welcome the children and tell them that you are going to tell them a story – a story that lots of them will know.

Explain that you will be needing eight volunteers to help you tell the story, and they must pretend to do whatever you tell them to do in the story. Then choose the children for each character, one by one, and place the correct label round each child's neck – make sure they know which character they are playing. Can they guess the story yet?

Show the child who will be playing the old man how to mime pulling something from the ground.

All the characters should sit in a line until they are called for in the story. Now you can start.

The tale of the enormous turnip

Once upon a time there was an old man and an old woman. With them lived a little boy and a little girl, a dog, a cat, a duck and a mouse.

Now the little old man liked to grow vegetables in his garden – beans and peas, potatoes and carrots, tomatoes and turnips. For a long time, all the vegetables grew normally, but one year, something very odd happened to one of his turnips. It started growing bigger and bigger, until it was taking up nearly all the space in one of the vegetable beds.

One morning, the old man went out to his garden to see how it was getting on. 'That looks just about big enough now,' he thought to himself. 'It'll make lots of lovely turnip soup.' And he grabbed the enormous turnip by its leaves and began to pull it out of the ground. (*Call the 'old man', and ask him to pretend to try to pull an imaginary turnip out of the ground – remind him how if necessary. The other characters will soon pick up what you want them to do, so they will need less explanation.*)

But the turnip stayed, stuck fast in the vegetable bed. So he called to the old woman in the house to come and help him to pull up the turnip. (*He beckons to the 'old woman' to come forward at this point.*) The old woman held onto the old man around his waist, and the old man grabbed the enormous turnip by its leaves. Then together they tried to pull it out of the ground. Still the turnip stayed, stuck fast in the vegetable bed. So the old man and the old woman called to the little boy to come and help them to pull up the turnip. (*They beckon to the 'little boy' to come forward.*)

The little boy held onto the old woman around her waist, the old woman held onto the old man around his waist, and the old man grabbed onto the enormous turnip by its leaves. Then together they tried to pull it out of the ground. But still the turnip stayed, stuck fast in the vegetable bed. So the old man, the old woman and the little boy called to the little girl to come and help them to pull up the turnip. (*They beckon to the 'little girl' to come forward.*)

The little girl held onto the little boy around his waist, the little boy held onto the old woman around her waist, the old woman held onto the old man around his waist, and the old man grabbed onto the enormous turnip by its leaves. Then together they tried to pull it out of the ground. But still the turnip stayed, stuck fast in the vegetable bed. So the old man, the old woman, the little boy and the little girl called to the dog to come and help them to pull up the turnip. (*They beckon to the 'dog' to come forward.*)

The dog held onto the little girl around her waist, the little girl held onto the little boy around his waist, the little boy held onto the old woman around her waist, the old woman held onto the old man around his waist, and the old man grabbed onto the enormous turnip by its leaves. Then together they tried to pull it out of the ground. But still the turnip stayed, stuck fast in the vegetable bed. So the old man, the old woman, the little boy, the little girl and the dog called to the cat to come and help them to pull up the turnip. (*They beckon to the 'cat' to come forward.*)

The cat held onto the dog around his waist, the dog held onto the little girl around her waist, the little girl held onto the little boy around his waist, the little boy held onto the old woman around her waist, the old woman held onto the old man around his waist, and the old man grabbed onto the enormous turnip by its leaves. Then together they tried to pull it out of the ground. But still the turnip stayed, stuck fast in the vegetable bed. So the old man, the old woman, the little boy, the little girl, the cat and the dog called to the duck to come and help them to pull up the turnip. (*They beckon to the 'duck' to come forward.*)

The duck held onto the cat by her waist, the cat held onto the dog around his waist, the dog held onto the little girl around her waist, the little girl held onto the little boy around his waist, the little boy held onto the old woman around her waist, the old woman held onto the old man around his waist, and the old man grabbed onto the enormous turnip by its leaves. Then together they tried to pull it out of the ground. But still the turnip stayed, stuck fast in the vegetable bed. So the old man, the old woman, the little boy, the little girl, the cat, the dog and the duck called to the mouse to come and help them to pull up the turnip. (*They beckon to the 'mouse' to come forward.*)

The mouse held onto the duck around his waist, the duck held onto the cat around her waist, the cat held onto the dog around his waist, the dog held onto the little girl around her waist, the little girl held onto the little boy around his waist, the little boy held onto the old woman around her waist, the old woman held onto the old man around his waist, and the old man grabbed onto the enormous turnip by its leaves. Then together they tried to pull it out of the ground. They tugged and they pulled, and they pulled and they tugged. There was a creaking and a groaning, and then with a loud 'Pop!' the enormous turnip came out of the vegetable bed and landed on the ground in front of them. (*Make sure that this next bit is done really carefully so that none of the children get hurt – you may need to stop the children from actually sitting on top of one another as happens in the original story.*)

The old man was so surprised that he nearly landed on the old woman; the old woman was so surprised that she nearly landed on the little boy; the little boy was so surprised that he nearly landed on the little girl; the little girl was so surprised that she nearly landed on the dog; the dog was so surprised that he nearly landed on the cat; the cat was so surprised that she nearly landed on the duck; and the duck was so surprised that he nearly landed on the little mouse.

They lay there for a few moments to get their breath back, then they all went home to make some lovely turnip soup.

Who do you think actually made the difference in pulling up the turnip?

(*Ask some children to tell you who they think, and why. Then stand the story characters in a line starting with the old man, and ask each child to take their label off and turn it around. Read the word that is made – TOGETHER. Then continue.*)

None of the characters in the story was strong enough to pull the enormous turnip out of the vegetable bed by themselves. Each one of them helped in a little way, and it was because they all worked together that the turnip came out of the ground.

Reflection

None of the people in the story was afraid to ask the others to help them with something that was too hard for them to do by themselves. In the same way, we can do some things better when we let other people help us – when we co-operate, or work together. There is a saying that grown-ups use that goes like this: 'A problem shared is a problem halved.' This is another way of saying that when we ask someone else to help us with a difficult problem, the problem becomes easier for us to work out because we work it out together.

Some people who believe in God will often ask him to help them with difficult things.

Let's have a few quiet moments now to think or pray ... .

Prayer

Dear God,
There are times when we struggle with difficult things, things we can't manage
by ourselves.
Thank you that we can call upon our friends to help us.

Amen.

Suggestions for music

First movement from *Serenade in G* by Mozart

'The frog chorus' by Paul McCartney

Promises

Introduction

This assembly is relatively quick and easy to prepare and can once again make use of children's thoughts if you prefer. I used this assembly originally to introduce the children to reasons why people make New Year's resolutions, but I have adapted it here just to illustrate what a promise is and what it means to make a promise. The game that is used is similar in design to the broken heart game.

Resources

- seven pieces of A4 paper in a colour of your choice
- letters cut out of paper – P, R, O, M, I, S, E
- at least six pieces of card in different colours.

Timing

15–20 minutes

Preparation

On each of the pieces of coloured A4 paper, stick a different letter of the word 'PROMISE'.

Now discuss the following with your class, or think up your own ideas if you prefer.

- do they know what a promise is?
- what does it mean to make a promise?
- when do people make promises?

From the discussion, choose seven sentences – one for each letter of the word 'PROMISE'. I chose sentences such as:

- When you make a promise, you must really mean it.
- When you make a promise, you must try to keep it.
- If you break a promise, people will be sad.
- You can make promises to your friends.
- When people get married they make promises to one another.
- Rainbows and Brownies make promises.

You may need to ask probing questions to help the discussion along. When you have seven suitable sentences, write them out and stick a different one on the back of each of the letters.

Now ask the children for some promises that either they have made, or people have made to them. (Or again, you can write your own.) Write a few of the best (about six is ideal) on the pieces of coloured card. Then 'break' the promises by cutting them in half along a zig-zag line so that no two pieces look the same.

Either select seven children from your class to read the phrases in assembly, or choose seven children from those in the hall.

If you intend to use this assembly to focus on New Year's resolutions, some children could also think of things that they would like to do better in the coming year – we wrote ours on 'think' bubbles and those children who wanted to share them with others read them out.

The Assembly

(Welcome the children and explain that we are going to be thinking about something quite important in assembly today, and you will be needing some helpers later on to help sort out some puzzles.

Choose seven children, and give them a letter each (in order) then ask them to stand in a line and look at the word – ask if anyone can read what the word says. Then explain that on the back of each letter is a thought about promises. As each phrase is read and turned round for all to see, discuss what is written there with the children. Then continue.)

All those sentences that we have just read help us to think about promises and what it means to make a promise. Some people believe that making a promise is a really serious thing to do. It's a difficult thing to try to keep a promise – sometimes we forget what we have said, or we change our minds. It's so easy to break a promise, but much harder to keep one. Some people think that you must only say 'I promise' if you really, really mean it and you are going to try hard to make the promise come true.

Now I have a few puzzles here that have got a little bit muddled up. On each puzzle is a promise, and at the moment, they are all broken. They are all about promises that we might make to other people at some point in our lives, or that other people might make to us.

I need some helpers to come and take a piece of puzzle. (*Choose as many children as you have pieces of puzzle.*) Now, can you find the other piece of puzzle that goes with yours and put the promise back together? Let's have a look at what each one says.

(*Talk about each promise briefly.*)

Reflection

I'd like us to have a few quiet moments to think about what we have heard today, when you can either pray or think. Some people believe that if they ask God, he will help them to do really difficult things like keeping promises.

Prayer

Dear God,
We have been thinking today about what it means to make a promise.
We can make promises for all sorts of reasons.
Promises can be hard to keep – help us, we pray.

Amen.

Suggestions for music

'Largo' from *Symphony no. 9 in E minor (The New World)* by Dvorak

Desert island discs

Introduction

This assembly started off as part of a class discussion: often a good place to start. It is an alternative version of the famous radio show – except that children choose to bring with them the most precious thing that they have. The only preparation it requires is for the children to have considered, and brought in (if they can!) their precious thing. It is a good way of helping children think about the fact that it is not the monetary worth of something that makes it precious, but the value that an individual places on an object. Just because you don't consider something to be precious does not mean that it is not important to somebody else. This concept is a good foundation for understanding and appreciating what others believe.

A wonderful follow-up to this assembly for another day is to read *Wilfred Gordon McDonald Partridge* by Mem Fox (published by Picture Puffins ISBN 0–14–050586–5).

Resources

- a picture of a desert island
- your class's precious objects (or drawings of them if they cannot be brought into school)
- a recording of the *Desert Island Discs* theme tune (not essential, but fun)
- a Bible, or you could use a Qur'an or replica Torah scroll instead. (Care needs to be taken with the handling of a Qur'an – hands must be washed and the Qur'an must be placed on a table or stand, not the floor. It is usually only opened to be read, not for display purposes. When it is not being used, it should be kept wrapped up.)

Timing

15 minutes

Preparation

Explain to your class what a desert island is, using the picture to help, and that you want them to pretend that they are going on a visit to one. Tell them that they are only allowed to take one thing with them – the most precious thing that they have.

Ask them to think what that precious thing would be – the one, special thing that they would really miss if they did not have it with them.

Then play the circle game with your class – pass a shell, stone, coconut, or something else that would fit in with the desert island theme – around the circle, and each child says, 'If I went to a desert island, I would take ... ' then finishes the sentence off by saying what their precious thing is. It helps the children if you start the ball rolling – be prepared!

It's also good to go around the circle again, so that each child can say why their object is so precious to them – be ready for some quite unusual answers.

Select some children to help you in the assembly. Ask them to bring in their precious objects on the assembly day – if they are allowed. If not, ask them to draw a picture of it to show instead.

The Assembly

(Welcome the children and then show the picture of the desert island, explaining how lonely it would be there on your own. Then continue.)

Some grown-ups listen to a radio show called 'Desert Island Discs'. Famous people are invited to be on the show and tell everyone who is listening what songs or pieces of music they would take with them to listen to while they are on the desert island. My class had its own desert island discs show in our classroom and we should like to share it with you. We didn't choose music or songs though – we each chose the most precious thing that we had to take with us.

(Play the theme tune, and then repeat the circle game – except it's more helpful if the children stand in a line, and less distracting if they speak in turn without the use of the shell, stone or coconut. As each child takes a turn, ask them to explain to everyone why their precious object is so special to them. Then continue.)

All of us have things that we think are precious, things that mean a lot to us. Today we have seen a lot of different precious things. *(Name some of them and remind the children why they were precious.*) When we call something precious, we don't always mean that it is worth lots of money. You might look at something that is really precious to me and think, 'It doesn't look special,' or, 'It's old and dirty.' Whatever you might think about it, it is still precious to me. We need to remember this when we look at anything that belongs to somebody else – whatever it looks like. We would want others to take care of our precious thing, not because it looks valuable but just because it was special to us.

For people who are Christians (*You could add or exchange Jews or Muslims, depending on your audience.*) this book (*Show the Bible, Qur'an or replica Torah.*) might be one of their most precious objects. Does anyone know what it is?

That's right, it's a Bible (*Qur'an, replica Torah*). Now it doesn't look very different from any other book, but it is precious to a Christian (*Muslim, Jew*) because they read it to find out more about God. It tells them things that help them when they are sad, or afraid, or lonely, and reminds them of things that make them glad.

I'd like you to think now about something that is precious to you.

Reflection

Let's have a few quiet moments to think or pray.

We have been thinking today about precious things. We are glad that we have them to remind us of happy times, people we love and things that are important to us. When we see something that is not ours, may we remember that it might be precious to somebody else and treat it with care and respect.

Prayer

Dear God,
We have been thinking today about precious things. We are glad that we have them to remind us of happy times, people we love and things that are important to us. When we see something that is not ours, help us to remember that it might be precious to somebody else and treat it with care and respect.
Amen.

Suggestions for music

'By the sleepy lagoon' by Eric Coates (Theme from *Desert Island Discs*)

'Message in a bottle' by The Police

Watch what you say!

Introduction

This assembly is designed to tackle the all-too-familiar problem of helping children to understand that what we say may have a profound impact on other people. The assembly could be shortened by just using the 'demonstration' and the brief talk following it. It includes the option of involving your own class again.

Resources

- a tube of toothpaste, or an aerosol can (air freshener is ideal)
- paper cut into the shape of speech bubbles, or empty speech bubbles drawn onto OHP acetate
- OHP if using the second option.

Timing

10–15 minutes

Preparation

Ask your class to think of something that has been said to them which has really hurt them inside. If children are willing, you could also ask them to think of something that they have said which they know has hurt somebody else. For this assembly, focus the children on what people have said, not what they have done.

Ask them to write their suggestions inside the speech bubbles, or you can write for them if you prefer. The children can either read these out themselves, or you can ask for volunteers during the assembly.

If you are not going to use your class, you will need to prepare the OHP acetate.

The Assembly _____

(Welcome the children and explain that today we are going to be thinking about what we say – our words. If you want to make the assembly shorter, skip over this next part, and go straight to the talk.

Otherwise, continue by explaining that your class have helped to think of things that others have said to them that have hurt them, and ask your children to read, or let you read, what is written on their speech bubbles. If you are not using your class, you will have to ask for suggestions from the children in the hall, and write one inside each speech bubble.

After each one, ask the children what the person who upset that child should have said. Now continue with the talk.)

I need someone to help me at the front please. *(Choose a suitable volunteer – it will need to be someone who won't mind being given an impossible task – and give them the toothpaste tube or aerosol can.)*

Can you tell the other children what I've given you?

I want you to take the top off and give the toothpaste *(or can)* a squeeze *(or spray)*.

(This will probably create a bit of a stir – so be prepared to calm everyone before you carry on!)

Now, I want you to put the toothpaste *(or air freshener)* back. Can you do it?

I have given you a rather impossible job, haven't I? Once the toothpaste *(or air freshener)* has left the tube *(or can)*, it's very difficult, if not impossible to get it back in again.

Let's give _____ a big clap for trying so hard. *(Invite them to return to their place, then continue.)*

Just as it's very, very difficult to put toothpaste back into its tube *(or air freshener into its can)*, it's the same with the words that we say. Once we have opened our mouths and let out the words, we can't get them back again. All of us sometimes say things that afterwards we wish we hadn't, because they have upset somebody or got us into trouble.

Reflection

Let's have a few quiet moments to think on what we have talked about this morning.

It says in the Bible that you are wise if you think before you speak.

This means that before we say anything, we should think hard about whether it will hurt anyone's feelings. This is a hard thing to do. People who are Christians, who read the Bible and try to do what it says, believe that if they ask God, he will help them. Let us think quietly for a moment about times when we might have said hurtful things to someone.

Prayer

Dear God,
We are sorry that we sometimes say things that make other people unhappy.
Please help us to think before we speak.

Amen.

Suggestions for music

'It's not what you do, it's the way that you do it' by Fun Boy Three

Forgiveness

Introduction

This is a very quick assembly, intended to explain to children what forgiveness really means. It involves a short talk, using letters to spell key words, and it is well worth practising beforehand – juggling letters is not easy!

Resources

- two large pieces of card in different colours.

Timing

5–10 minutes

Preparation

Cut out each of the letters of the word 'FORGIVENESS' in one colour of card.

Cut eleven cards from the other colour to mount the letters.

The letter cards are for a simple explanation of what 'forgiveness' means.

The Assembly

(Welcome the children and then ask for eleven volunteers to hold up some letters – they must stand up or move or turn letters round when you want them to.

Give each child a letter of the word 'forgiveness' and stand them in a line – the letters shouldn't be showing at this point. The idea is to use the individual cards to spell new words that will help your explanation.)

We are going to be thinking today about a very long word, that is quite hard to explain – let's look at it now. *(All the children turn their letters round.)* It says 'forgiveness'. *(Ask the children to turn the letters back again.)*

(Collect children with the letters S, I and N and stand them in front.) Each of us do things that hurt other people – another word for this which some people use is ... *(Ask these children to turn their letters round.)* 'sin'.

(Return the children to their correct places and collect children with the letters G, I, V and E, and stand them in front.)

Forgiveness means that when people do or say things that hurt us, even though they have done something wrong, we will ... *(Ask these children to turn their letters round.)* 'give' them another chance.

(Return the children to their correct places and collect children with the letters N, E, V, E and R, and stand them at the front.)

Forgiveness also means that we will ... *(Ask these children to turn their letters round.)* 'never' remind them of what they did that upset or hurt us. It is as if it never happened.

(Ask all the children to return to their places before you continue.*)*

Reflection

Each of us can do things that hurt other people – often without really meaning to. It makes the person we have hurt feel better if we show that we are sorry about what we have done, and tell them that we are.

But forgiving someone who has hurt us is not an easy thing to do. We may not feel like forgiving them – especially if they don't sound as if they are sorry. But people usually feel lots better inside when we really forgive someone for the hurt they have done to us.

When someone hurts us, may we try to be people who are ready to forgive.

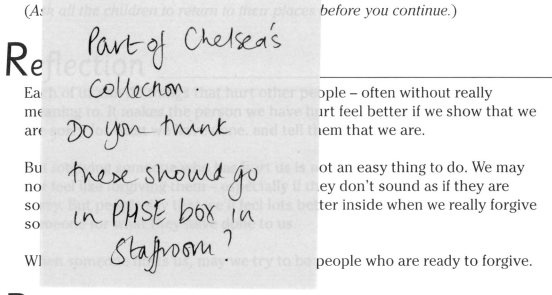

Part of Chelsea's collection. Do you think these should go in PHSE box in staffroom?

Prayer

Dear God,
Each of us can do things that hurt other people – often without really meaning to.
Help us to be truly sorry, and tell them that we are.
When someone hurts us, please help us to forgive them.

Amen.

Suggestions for music

'On your shore' from *Watermark* by Enya

Letters to God

Introduction

This assembly is designed to introduce children to the concept of prayer – we need to make sure that children understand what they are doing since, in assemblies, we often ask them to pray. The assembly is quick and easy to prepare for, and can include children's work if desired.

Resources

- a variety of letters – e.g. postcard, letter, invitation, thank you letter etc. – you could almost just bring in your morning mail!
- paper for writing on, if you want to include children's work.

Timing

10–15 minutes

Preparation

If you intend using your class, you will need to discuss the various forms of letter with them first. Then ask them, 'If you could write a letter to God, what would you tell him or ask him?' Some children may not wish to participate in this activity, in which case they should not be asked to do so.

The children could write their letters down to read out in assembly if they want to. Then collect together the material for your assembly, and you are ready!

The Assembly

(Welcome the children to the assembly and explain that today you are going to be thinking about what a prayer is – using some letters to help you.

Show them the different letters that you have brought with you, and discuss the many different formats and what they are for. You could involve children by choosing one at a time to pick a letter to show the other children, and ask questions about it, such as, 'Why would someone choose to send a postcard?' Look at the way of addressing the letter too, since this will come up later in the assembly. Then continue.)

When we want to tell things to people who live in a different place from us, we might write them a letter. All those letters I showed you were ways of telling people things. Sometimes we may need to give people important information about a special event, like a birthday party. Sometimes we may want to send a postcard to tell them about a lovely place that we've visited. Sometimes we may want to write to say thank you to someone, or to say that we are sorry about something. Sometimes, we might just want to write to someone to ask how they are.

We are going to think about prayer for a few minutes now. Saying a prayer is really just like writing a letter – it's telling somebody something. When people talk about praying, who might they be praying to? (*Ask a few children.*)

When people say prayers, they are talking to God about things. Just like the letters we looked at, there are lots of different things that people who pray want to tell or ask God.

(*Omit this next section if you are not involving your class.*)

I asked [some of] my children what they would write to God about. Here's what they said.

(*Ask them to read out their letters.*)

All sorts of people pray, for all sorts of reasons. People who are Christians, Jews, Muslims, Hindus or Sikhs (*Choose which religious are appropriate for your school.*) all say prayers – sometimes they make the prayers up themselves, sometimes they use prayers that other people have written down.

Christians sometimes use a special prayer, called 'The Lord's Prayer', which Jesus taught to his special friends. It tells God that they think he is special, and asks God to help them in their everyday lives. Christians believe that when they talk to God, he will listen. They talk to God as if they are writing him a letter – sometimes they might ask God for things that they need, or tell him that he is really important to them. They might say thank you for something good that has happened to them, or ask him for help when they don't know what to do. They might pray for someone they know who is sick, and ask God to make them better. Anyone can pray – anywhere or at any time.

Reflection

We have been thinking today about prayer – talking to God. May we remember that we can pray at any time, in any place, whatever the reason.

Let's have a few quiet moments now – you can say your own prayer if you like. Then I'm going to use a short prayer that you can make your own by saying 'Amen' at the end if you want to.

Prayer

Dear God,
Please give us today the things that we really need and help us to make right choices in everything we do.

Amen.

Suggestions for music

'Isn't it amazing' from *Songs from the rain* by Hothouse Flowers

Beautiful inside

Introduction

In the western world today, we are finding that more and more emphasis is placed on being attractive on the outside. This assembly uses the story of The Ugly Duckling to help children to understand that everyone is beautiful in their own way, even if they don't think that they are. It requires very little preparation.

Resources

- some large photographs or posters of different faces.

Include faces with lots of different characters – old, young, all skin tones, 'models' and 'ordinary' people. Small photographs can be used to quite good effect by having them photocopied onto OHP acetate at a printing shop, if the school does not have a colour photocopier. If you can find a copy of the song 'The Ugly Duckling', by Danny Kaye, this could take the place of the story.

Timing

15 minutes

Preparation

Collect the resources outlined above – there is no set order that the photographs should be shown in.

The Assembly

(Welcome the children and tell them that you want them to look at some different people's faces.

Show the faces one by one, leaving them on view for a short time before moving on to the next – it is not necessary at this stage to make any comments. Then tell the children that you are going to show them the faces again, and this time they must decide which ones are beautiful faces – ask the children to indicate by raising their hands. Ask a few children whose hands are up to explain what is beautiful about the face if they can – it's not always easy to put into words even as an adult! Then continue.)

All of you had different ideas about which of those faces were beautiful, and you all had different reasons for choosing. Everyone has their own idea about what a 'beautiful' person should look like. But everyone is beautiful in their own way – no matter what they look like.

The story we're going to hear today is all about a little duckling, who believed he was ugly.

The story of the ugly duckling

On the edge of a river bank, just beneath some reeds, five eggs were beginning to hatch. The mother duck had been sitting on them for some time now, waiting for this moment to come. One by one the eggs developed cracks, then, one by one, little beaks started to push the cracks open. Then, one at a time, the egg shells split – one, two, three, four little yellow ducklings. At last the final shell started to crack open and there amongst the broken bits of shell sat a rather exhausted and bedraggled little duckling. He wasn't quite the same yellow colour as the others, but the mother duck didn't seem to mind.

Straight away, she led her new babies to the edge of the water and into the river in a little line. The days went by, and the little ducklings grew and grew. They loved to splash and chase each other in the water, but they soon began to realize that the duckling who hatched last was different from them, and they would tease him and make fun of him, saying, 'Quack! Quack! Quack! You're not like us – your feathers are all brown. What an ugly duckling you are. Quack! Quack! Quack!'

Soon, the little duckling felt so ashamed that he didn't want to swim with his brothers and sisters any more, so he would go off by himself to explore the reeds further down the river. There were other families of ducks who lived there, and he often asked if he could join in their games, but they, too, said, 'Quack! Quack! Quack! Your feathers are all brown – what an ugly duckling you are. We don't want you playing with us. Quack! Quack! Quack!'

Sad, and feeling very alone, the little duckling swam off. He looked back at the other ducklings, splashing and playing, and a tear rolled down his beak and plopped into the water. 'I must be so ugly,' he thought to himself. 'Nobody wants me to play with them. I hate having brown feathers – how I wish they were yellow like all the other ducklings.' And off he swam, wanting to be far, far away from the other ducklings because he felt so ugly.

Days went by, and he got used to being by himself, searching in the reeds and at the bottom of the river for food to eat, and watching the other river life going about its business. But whenever he saw other duck families, he would always swim away from them, because he didn't want to hear from them how ugly he was.

Then one day, when he was busy searching in the grass along the river bank for his lunch, he saw the most wonderful sight that he had ever seen. Swimming towards him were some graceful, white birds who seemed to glide across the water as if they were skating on ice. He was so captivated by their beauty that he forgot to swim away, and as they got closer, one of the smaller birds bent its graceful, long neck to speak to him. 'Hello,' it said. 'Who are you, and how do you come to be swimming alone?' So the ugly duckling told his story about how the other ducklings in his part of the river had made fun of him and told him how ugly and brown his feathers were. 'But they're not brown, and you're not ugly,' said the beautiful white bird. 'But I am!' said the duckling. 'The others said that I was!'

'Take a look at yourself – you're one of us now.' And rather nervously, the duckling moved a little closer to the water's edge so that he could see his reflection in the river. He fully expected to see himself as he had been, with ugly brown feathers, but when he looked he gasped in surprise. Reflected in the water, he could see a white bird, with a long graceful neck, and he almost couldn't believe his eyes. He was not a duckling at all, but a beautiful swan!

Reflection

In the story, the little duckling with the brown feathers was told that he was ugly because he was different from all the others. Actually, he was different from them because he was a swan, and swan babies (called cygnets) do have feathers that are brown. He was not ugly at all – but he was made to feel ugly because of what the ducklings said to him.

Everyone is beautiful in their own way. No matter what we look like, we are still beautiful – beautiful on the inside. I often see children doing beautiful things, such as looking after someone else when they have fallen down, or making sure a new child in their class has someone to play with at playtime. When we show other people that we care about them, it makes them feel beautiful inside.

Let's have a few quiet moments now to think about what we have heard.

Prayer

Dear God,

It says in the Bible that you see what we are like on the inside. You see how we behave towards others, what we say to others, what we think about others. Please help us to become more beautiful on the inside by showing that we care about other people.

Help us to say and do things that will cause others to feel good about themselves.

Amen.

Suggestions for music

'The Ugly Duckling' by Danny Kaye

The hardest word

Introduction

How often have you heard a child say that they are sorry for doing something that has hurt or upset someone, only to witness them doing a similar thing not long afterwards? This assembly creates the opportunity to reflect on the fact that saying sorry and meaning it is a lot more difficult than it looks. This assembly requires a minimum of preparation, and is quite short.

Resources

- an overhead projector
- OHP acetate (or paper and pencil if the OHP is not an option)
- paper to cover the OHP.

Timing

10 minutes

Preparation

Write the following list of words onto the OHP acetate, one under another – or you could ask your children to think of words that get progressively harder to read or say, ending with 'sorry':

I; a; it; and; was; saw; what; went; looked; wanted; classroom; difficult; knee; dinosaur; adventure; spaghetti (guaranteed to tax the pronunciation!); surprisingly; sorry

You will also need a piece of paper to reveal the words one at a time to be read. The children will probably think you are a bit odd to start with, since some of the words are quite easy to say or read.

The Assembly

(Welcome the children and explain that you have a game to start off the assembly for which will need their help. Tell the children that you have made a list of words that get more and more difficult to say, and that you will show the words one at a time.)

Reveal the words one at a time, and ask for volunteers to read what the word says. When 'sorry' has been read out, continue.)

'Sorry' may not have been the most difficult word to read on our list, or even to pronounce – but I think that it is one of the hardest words to say. There have been many times when I've seen children saying 'sorry' for upsetting someone, and then I've watched them do the same thing again later on.

When we say 'sorry' to people, we should really mean that we will do our best not to hurt or upset them again. That's a difficult thing to do – to say sorry and mean that we are sorry.

Reflection

Everyone says or does things that they are sorry for – sometimes we do things by accident. It makes the person we've hurt or upset feel better when we apologize to them, and it makes us feel better inside, too. Being sorry means that we feel sad that we have upset someone and that we will try not to do it again.

People who are Christians believe that God is sad if he sees them hurting or upsetting another person. They believe that they need to say sorry to God, too.

Let's have a few quiet moments now to think about being sorry, and really meaning that we're sorry. Perhaps you'd like to make a little promise to yourself that the next time you say sorry, you will really mean it.

Prayer

Dear God,
We are sorry for all the times when we have hurt or upset other people –
sometimes by accident, sometimes on purpose. Help us to say sorry and really
mean that we are sorry.

Amen.

Suggestions for music

'Sorry seems to be the hardest word' by Elton John or Joe Cocker
(Album: *Two Rooms*)

Money, money, money

Introduction

In our world today, more and more emphasis is being placed on the importance of material possessions, and it is good to give children the opportunity to realize that for some people (Sikhs, in this case), money is not the be all and end all. This is a very quick and easy assembly to prepare. You can use children's written work, or just their verbal responses.

Resources

- copies of the 'money bags' for children to write their responses on– not needed if you are going to use verbal responses only.

Timing

15—20 minutes depending on the number of children you use in the assembly

Preparation

Ask your class this question:

'If someone gave you some money, what would you spend it on?'

Encourage the children to think carefully, and emphasize that they can spend the money on themselves or on someone else if they wish – the choice is theirs. When they have thought, choose someone to start, using the words, 'I would buy … '. If you prefer to have children reading out their work in assembly, they can record their responses on the 'money bags' sheets.

Choose a few children, with a range of responses, to read out or repeat their response in assembly – especially those who chose to spend the money on someone other than themselves.

The Assembly _____

(Play the first piece of music – suggested on page 50 – as the children are coming into the hall. When everyone has settled, welcome the children to assembly and ask if anyone could guess from the music what today's assembly might be about. Then continue.)

That's right, the song is called 'Money, money, money' and it talks about the many different things that can be done with a little money. During the week, I asked my class to think about what they would buy if someone gave them some money. Here's what they said.

(Ask the children you have chosen to read out or repeat their responses, discussing them a little if necessary, especially those who chose to spend on someone else. Then continue.)

The story I'm going to read to you is all about what a little boy did with some money he was given by his father. This little boy's name was Nanak, and he grew up to be a very wise man. Sikhs call him Guru Nanak because he spent his life teaching people about God.

The story of how Nanak spent his money

From the day that he was born, Nanak's parents knew that he was different from other children, and throughout his childhood he did many things that puzzled them. I expect some of you have heard your parents say to you, 'Why on earth did you do that?' and the same was often true of Nanak. But there was one day that really stuck in his father's memory – the day that he had given Nanak some money to spend in the town. 'Use this money wisely,' he had said to Nanak, thinking that his son would perhaps use it to make more money. At that time, he little knew what would happen ...

Nanak took the money from his father and set off for the town with his friend Bala. Part of their journey took them through a forest, and it was in this forest that some holy men were staying. These men spent their lives travelling around, learning about and teaching others about God, and so they did not have homes to live in. Nanak was very interested in how they managed without a home like he had, so he asked them, 'How do you manage to live in this forest with no homes, or money?' The holy men replied that they believed that God would always provide them with the things that they needed. 'But how long is it since you have had any food to eat?' Nanak asked. 'We have not had any food for four days now,' the holy men told him.

Nanak's face lit up. He started running towards the town, urging the holy men not to leave until he returned, and calling to Bala to follow him. Bala was naturally rather confused by what had happened and asked Nanak where he was going and why they were in such a hurry. 'I have decided what I shall spend my father's money on,' Nanak replied. 'Wait and see!'

When they got to town, Nanak wasted no time. He bought as much food as he could with the money his father had given him, much to Bala's dismay. 'Remember what your father said about spending the money wisely,' he kept reminding Nanak, but Nanak just kept buying more and more food. The holy men were still waiting when they returned to the forest. Nanak gave them the food and said, 'God has provided you with food once more.' The holy men were delighted with what Nanak had brought for them, and praised God for this boy who had performed such an act of kindness, but Bala had a very odd feeling about what Nanak had done. 'You will make your father very angry when you tell him what you have spent his money on,' Bala said to his friend as they walked home.

And Bala was right. Nanak's father was indeed angry when he heard what his money had been spent on, but Nanak couldn't understand why. 'I used the money to do the will of God,' he said. 'I would have thought that would be the best possible use for it.'

Reflection

In the story, the little boy Nanak used his father's money to help other people. The way that Nanak chose to live his life has helped many Sikhs to understand more about God. Sharing money with people who don't have much is a very important part of their lives.

Some of us may not have enough money to share, but many of us do. It's good for us to think about ways that our money can be used to help other people – by buying presents for people, or putting money in collection boxes when people come to our doors. It's good to have money to spend, but we need to remember that there are many other things in life that can make us happy. Most of the beautiful things in the world around us cannot be bought with any amount of money. Think of how wonderful the world seems when there is new snow on the ground, or when the sun comes out after many days of rain, or when there is a rainbow in the sky. None of these things can be bought with money, but how rich they make us feel! I'd like us to share a few quiet moments now to think, and pray if you would like to.

Prayer

Dear God,

We are grateful when we have money to spend. Please help us not to waste it, but to use it wisely, maybe to help someone else.

But we are also glad that our world is so full of other beautiful things, which money cannot buy – thank you God.

Amen.

Suggestions for music

'Money, money, money' by ABBA

'The sun that shines across the sea', traditional (to sing)

I would buy

New beginnings

Introduction

Jewish New Year (*Rosh Hashanah*) is usually celebrated around September, although the exact date changes from year to year, much like Easter. The idea of looking back over the old year and forward to the new is not dissimilar to the concept of New Year resolutions which we sometimes make on 1 January. This assembly is designed to introduce children to the way Jewish people celebrate *Rosh Hashanah,* and gives them an opportunity to reflect on what can be learnt from it.

Resources

- four pieces of card – large enough so that a word can be written on them for children to be able to see

You will only need the next two items if you are presenting this assembly to a relatively small group of children, or your assembly could last all day.

- apples cut up into small, bite-sized pieces, one piece for each child
- some honey in a bowl.

Timing

10–15 minutes

Preparation

On each piece of card write a different term from the following list:

Rosh Hashanah; teshuvah; tefillah; tzedakah

Then on the reverse side, write or draw the following:

Rosh Hashanah	*Leshanah tovah*	(This means 'For a good year' and is how Jewish people will greet each other at New Year.)
teshuvah	Draw a sad face.	

tefillah	Prayer
tzedakah	Draw a smiling face.

These will be used to form the outline of your assembly.

If children are going to sample apples dipped in honey, cut the apples into bite-sized pieces and cover them with clingfilm until they are needed, to prevent them from going too brown.

Before the assembly, you will need to make sure that the cards are placed face-up, with the words showing – *Rosh Hashanah; teshuvah; tefillah; tzedakah.*

The Assembly

(Welcome the children and explain that today is a special day for Jewish people. If the assembly is not held on the exact day, explain when it was. Tell them that it is Jewish New Year – Rosh Hashanah – *and hold up the card showing those words.)*

These words mean 'the head of the year' and it is a time when Jewish people remember the birthday of the human race. We celebrate New Year on 1 January each year – Jewish people celebrate their New Year, which they call *Rosh Hashanah,* in our month of September. Today we are going to find out some more about *Rosh Hashanah* and think about what it means to Jewish people.

I have some more cards here that will help us in our assembly – they have some other Jewish words written on them. Who'd like to come and choose one?

(Choose a child to select a word – and perhaps try to sound the word out as well. After each word has been read out, ask the child to turn the card around to show the picture. Then explain what it means.)

teshuvah (sad face)   At *Rosh Hashanah,* Jewish people will think hard about themselves, and what sort of person they are. They will think about the times when they have hurt someone and needed to say sorry, or times when they knew that they needed to do something good, but didn't. They will also say sorry to God for the wrong things they have done.

tefillah ('Prayer')   At *Rosh Hashanah,* Jewish people will go to the synagogue, which is their place of worship, and spend extra time praying to God, saying sorry for all the wrong things they have done, and praying that they will try to be better in the new year. At the special service a horn, called a shofar, made out of an animal horn, will be blown many times.

tzedakah (happy face)   Jewish people will think hard about the good things that they should try to do for other people in the new year.

(*Then look at the words that are written on the reverse of the* Rosh Hashanah *card. Explain them to the children.*)

This is how Jewish people will greet, or say hello, to each other at *Rosh Hashanah.* The words *'Leshanah tovah'* mean 'For a good year', so Jewish people will be saying that they want their friends and family to have a good year in the new year.

Jewish people celebrate the start of the new year by having special family meals, and they eat apples dipped in honey. The sweetness of the honey reminds them that they wish the new year to be sweet.

Reflection

We have been thinking today about how Jewish people celebrate *Rosh Hashanah.* It is important to them because it gives them time to say sorry for all the wrong things they have done, and reminds them to try harder to do good things in the new year.

It is good for us, too, to think about the sort of people that we have been and try harder to be better. Let's have a few quiet moments now to think whether there is anything that you have done or said yesterday, or even today, that has made someone else sad. Maybe you didn't say sorry when you should have done – you might like to decide to say sorry to that person when you next see them.

Prayer

Dear God,
Each one of us can do or say things that hurt other people – we are sorry.
Help us, today and every day, to try hard to be better, and to do good things.

Amen.

After the prayer, if your children are going to be sharing apples dipped in honey, explain how you are going to approach it.

To try to ease congestion, it may be helpful if you dip the apple pieces and give them to the children who want them – they have to go straight in their mouths to avoid sticky drips.

Suggestions for music

'Allegro' from *Clarinet concerto in A major* by Mozart

Sukkot

Introduction

The festival of *Sukkot* comes in the autumn and lasts a week. It has a twofold purpose – to celebrate the harvest, and to remind Jews today of how their ancestors lived in tents in the desert on their 40-year journey from Egypt to Israel. This assembly requires some preparation, but is well worth the effort – your class will need to help with the preparation beforehand. If building a *sukkah* (the shelter that Jews build during *Sukkot*) sounds too much of a challenge, the assembly could be delivered just using the story (with actions).

Resources

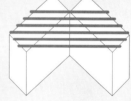

- two stage blocks, portable display boards or the sides of a role-play area
- some bamboo canes or wooden dowelling
- coloured paper for cutting out palms and fruit
- thread for attaching fruit to the ceiling of the *sukkah*
- Sellotape.

Timing

20–25 minutes

Preparation

Each Jewish family will build a *sukkah* in their garden for the duration of the festival. The roof has to be made of things that have been growing, so many will use branches and palm leaves. A gap must be left, big enough for the sky to be seen, and the inside will be decorated with fruit and pictures. You and your children are going to make your own *sukkah* in the assembly hall.

Before building your *sukkah,* ask your children to draw and cut out some fruit shapes from the coloured paper – they could cut lemons, oranges, apples, bananas, pears, and they need to make them about life-size. Attach a thread to each fruit – in the assembly, each child will bring one to you for hanging in the roof. They could also help you to cut out lots of large palm leaves which must be big enough to form the roof covering of the *sukkah.*

Before the assembly starts, you will need to put together the sides of the *sukkah* in the hall – the two blocks need to stand so that they meet at one corner in a V-shape. You will then need to secure bamboo canes so that they form a flat roof over the two sides. To make it safe, cut off any bamboo ends that jut out over the side of the *sukkah*.

The Assembly

(Welcome the children and explain that you will be doing something rather different in assembly today.)

At this time of year, lots of people will be celebrating the harvest – saying thank you to God for the fruit, vegetables and grain that they have grown. We are going to think about how Jewish people celebrate their harvest festival, which they call *Sukkot*. I have begun to build a shelter called a *sukkah*. A long time ago, the Jewish people had to make a very long journey. While they travelled, they lived in homes like tents that could be easily taken down so that they could move on to the next place. At *Sukkot*, Jewish people today build little shelters in their gardens to remind themselves of how people used to live, and how lucky they are to have proper homes. They will eat in their *sukkah* during the week when they celebrate harvest, and sometimes even sleep there!

Today you are going to help me to finish my *sukkah* – I have some palm leaves here to finish off the roof. We shall be celebrating harvest soon, so let's think about some of the food we are grateful for. As you fetch a palm leaf, you can tell me the food you are grateful for and we'll build the roof together. Who'd like to collect a palm leaf and help me?

(Choose a few children – not from your own class – to pass you a palm leaf, and build up the roof by laying palm leaves across the bamboo canes. The children could do this themselves if they are tall enough. Whilst the roof is being completed, continue.)

The roof is a very important part of the *sukkah,* and when Jewish people cover the roof with leaves and branches, they always leave a gap in the palm leaves so that they can see the sky.

(Ask a child to check whether they can see the hall ceiling through the sukkah.)

Now the roof is finished, we need to decorate the inside. My children need to help me now – as they bring their decorations, they will tell me about the food they are grateful for.

(As each child brings you their fruit shape on a thread, secure the thread to a bamboo cane and continue with the explanation as to why you are doing this.)

Many different types of fruit come from Israel, which is where lots of Jewish people live, and they hang real fruit from the roof of their *sukkah* to show that they are grateful to God for their harvest.

Now that our *sukkah* is complete, I'm going to read you a short story that Jewish people will tell each other during the festival of *Sukkot*. It has a few actions that you can join in with.

(Teach the children the following actions. Every time you say any of these words in the story, they must do the actions.

desert – draw one hand along an imaginary flat line

Egypt – point behind you

Promised Land – point straight ahead

complained – 'moan, moan, moan' (in a whining voice)

tents – use hands to make a flat roof over head

eat – pretend to eat with fingers

drink – pretend to drink

God – point upwards, as if to heaven

manna – hold fingers above head and do an action similar to how rain is simulated in action songs. Manna is what the Israelites called the bread-like substance that appeared with the dew each morning.

quails – hold hands at side to make small wings, and flap hands.)

This is a story that Jewish people remember at *Sukkot*. It tells of their journey with Moses, their leader, through the desert *(making a flat line with one hand)* from Egypt *(pointing behind)* to the Promised Land *(pointing ahead)*.

The Jewish people had escaped from being slaves in Egypt *(pointing behind)* and for a while they were happy to be free. But after a while, they began to complain *(moan, moan, moan)* about anything and everything. 'It's too hot!'

they complained (*moan, moan, moan*). 'We have hardly anything to eat!' (*pretending to eat*) they complained (*moan, moan, moan*). 'There is hardly any water for us to drink!' (*pretending to drink*) they complained (*moan, moan, moan*).

'Life is hard! At least in Egypt (*pointing behind*) we had plenty to eat (*pretending to eat*) and drink!'(*pretending to drink*) they complained (*moan, moan, moan*).

God (*pointing upwards*) heard what the Jewish people were saying to Moses. God (*pointing upwards*) told Moses, 'In the evenings, I will give my people meat to eat (*pretending to eat*) and in the mornings I will give them bread to eat (*pretending to eat*).'

And so, that night, when the Jewish people had put up their tents (*making flat roof over head*) an enormous flock of quails (*flapping wings*) landed near their tents (*making flat roof over head*). God (*pointing upwards*) had kept his promise and given them meat to eat (*pretending to eat*).

In the morning, when the people came out of their tents (*making flat roof over head*) there was a strange powdery substance on the ground, which they called 'manna' (*raining down with fingers*). They believed that the manna (*raining down with fingers*) fell from heaven.

Every day, the people collected the manna (*raining down with fingers*) – all except for one day in every week – *Shabbat. Shabbat* is a special day for Jews because God (*pointing upwards*) told them to rest on that day and do no work. No manna (*raining down with fingers*) fell on *Shabbat,* so God (*pointing upwards*) sent them twice as much manna (*raining down with fingers twice – twice as much*) the day before *Shabbat,* enough food for two days.

The Jewish people travelled in the desert (*making a flat line with one hand*), living in tents (*making flat roof over head*) for 40 years until they reached the Promised Land (*pointing ahead*). And each day, God (*pointing upwards*) would provide them with quails (*flapping wings*) in the evening and manna (*raining down with fingers*) in the morning.

That story tells us why the Jewish people celebrate *Sukkot* – as a reminder that God had provided food for them while they were in the desert travelling to Israel, the Promised Land, as they called it. *Sukkot* is a time for them to be thankful that they don't have to live in tents, or eat manna and quails all the time – a time to be thankful for their homes and for the food that they eat every day.

Reflection

Today we have thought why we are grateful for our food, too – let's have a few quiet moments to think about what we have heard. I shall be saying a prayer in a while. If you agree with what I am saying, you can join in with 'Amen' at the end.

Prayer

Dear God,
At this time when Jewish people all over the world are saying thank you for their homes and their harvest, we want to take a few moments now to say thank you, too. We are grateful that we don't have to live in tents, and that we have food to eat. Thank you God.

Amen

Suggestions for music

'All things bright and beautiful' (to sing)

Remember

Introduction

The subject of Remembrance Day is quite a difficult one to tackle with young children. Some people would consider that it is too morbid an occasion for school, but we believe that it is important that children are made aware, if only in a very small way, that their great-grandparents' generation were prepared to give their lives for the freedom of generations to come. This assembly requires a little preparation in advance – again, children's work can be used, or you can do your own if you are feeling artistic.

Resources

- eight pieces of white A4 paper
- red letters – R, E, M, E, M, B, E, R
- white paper, slightly smaller than A4 – see *Preparation* below.

Timing

15–20 minutes

Preparation

Stick each of the red letters on a piece of A4 paper.

On white paper, draw – or ask the children to draw or paint – a selection of pictures to show events that we regularly remember as part of the school year. The following list is just a selection – you could probably think of many more events relevant to your children's cultural background. What is important is that children will be able to recognize easily the event from the picture, so choose carefully! Select eight, *including the poppy*.

- a birthday cake or present – Birthdays
- a Christmas tree or present – Christmas
- an Easter egg – Easter
- large writing: '1 January' – New Year
- pancakes and lemons – Pancake Day
- a red heart – St Valentine's Day
- fireworks – Bonfire Night

- Chinese dragon – Chinese New Year
- diva lamp and sweets or rangoli patterns – Divali
- a large poppy – Remembrance Day

Now, for each sheet of paper with the red letters, stick one of the eight pictures on the reverse, so there is a letter on one side and a picture on the other. The poppy must be on the last letter R.

The Assembly

(Welcome the children and explain that we shall be thinking about some special days that we remember during the year. Choose eight children to hold the letters. Ask if anyone can read what the word says.

Then ask one child at a time to turn round their letter so that the picture can be seen, and invite children in the hall to guess which day is being remembered. As they guess, talk briefly about how each special day is remembered.

Children may not know which day the red poppy reminds us of, so it's worth spending a little time explaining it to them.)

Poppy Day, or Remembrance Day, is a sad day for lots of people. When your great-grandparents were growing up, before you or your mums and dads were born, there were two very big wars. Some of your great-grandparents may have gone to the wars to fight. The soldiers, sailors and airmen fighting for Britain won both the wars, but lots and lots of them were hurt, or even killed in these wars, and their families were very sad.

Each year since the end of World War I in 1918, people take time to remember those who died or were injured during the wars. Since the end of World War II, there have been other wars and more people have been killed.

Most of us at school today won't know anyone who fought in those wars, but for many people, it is a sad day. The special day when we remember those who fought for our country is always the second Sunday in November. People buy red poppies to wear, and lots of people will think for a few moments in silence about those who have died or been injured.

Reflection

I'd like us to close our eyes now and remember that many people gave their lives to keep our country safe from our enemies. (*This need only last for a few moments – then move on to the reflection or prayer.*)

In silence we have remembered those who were prepared to give their lives for the freedom of our country. As we grow up, may we try to make our world a more peaceful place to live in, free from war.

Prayer

Dear God,
We want to remember in these few moments of silence that in the wars that have been fought, there were many people who gave up their lives for our freedom. We are grateful to them, and to you, for keeping us safe since then. Keep our world a peaceful place, we pray.

Amen.

Suggestions for music

'Venus – Bringer of Peace' from *The Planets* by Gustav Holst

'Make me a channel of your peace', the prayer of St Francis of Assisi, arranged by Sebastian Temple (to sing)

Hanukkah

Introduction

This assembly is excellent for anyone who is prepared to include some actions. It requires no practical preparation, unless you wish to use your own class at the front to help with the actions. It can be used as a story in its own right, or as a reflection on why Jewish people celebrate *Hanukkah*. Be prepared for an assembly with rather more noise than usual.

Resources

If the story is being used as part of reflections on *Hanukkah,* it may be helpful to use a *hanukiah* (nine-branched candlestick lit at *Hanukkah*) as a visual aid, and light it for the children to see at the end.

Timing

20 minutes

The Assembly

(Welcome the children and introduce the theme of the assembly. Then teach the children the actions, explaining that they do them once, then return their hands to their laps to be ready for the next action. It may be worth trying a small section of the story so that the children have a chance to get used to being involved in this way.

Actions:
King Antiochus – 'Boo!'
Judah Maccabee – 'Hurray!'
soldiers – salute
read the Torah – open a scroll
eat – hands to lips
Jerusalem – point East with right hand
lamps – cup hands to look like a candle flame

Warn the children to watch out for some added actions as the story goes along. Now read the story.)

The story of Hanukkah

This is a story that Jewish people remember each year when they celebrate *Hanukkah.* It is the story of the Jewish people who lived in the city of Jerusalem (*pointing East with the right hand*), a good leader, Judah Maccabee (*'Hurray!'*), and a wicked king, Antiochus (*'Boo!'*).

Long ago, God gave the Jewish people rules to help them to live their lives. He told them to pray to him, to eat (*hands to lips*) special food, and to read the Torah (*open scroll*) where God's laws were written. The Torah (*open scroll*) was kept in the Temple, a special building in Jerusalem (*pointing East with the right hand*), where the Jews went to worship God. Because they loved God, the Jews kept God's laws. For a long time, everyone was happy (*draw a smile on face*).

Then a new king came to rule over the Jewish people. His name was King Antiochus (*'Boo!'*). He told the Jewish people that they were not allowed to eat (*hands to lips*) their special food, or read the Torah (*open scroll*). What was even worse, King Antiochus (*'Boo!'*) told them that they must not pray to God. What should they do? They were frightened of the soldiers (*salute*) but they loved God and went on keeping his laws. This made King Antiochus (*'Boo!'*) very cross (*'Grrr!!'*).

One day King Antiochus (*'Boo!'*) could stand it no more. He sent his soldiers (*salute*) into the Temple in Jerusalem (*pointing East with right hand*) and they ripped up the Torah (*open scroll*). Then the soldiers (*salute*) began to spoil all the other beautiful things there, and put out the special lamp (*cup hands*) that burned day and night in the Temple.

When they saw what the soldiers (*salute*) had done, the Jewish people were very sad (*unhappy face*). Judah Maccabee (*'Hurray!'*) gathered together just a few Jewish soldiers (*salute*) and went into the hills near where the soldiers (*salute*) of King Antiochus (*'Boo!'*) were camped. The soldiers (*salute*) of King Antiochus (*'Boo!'*) were strong and rode on elephants, but the Jewish soldiers (*salute*), although they were few, were fighting for what they believed in.

There were many battles, but finally the soldiers (*salute*) of Judah Maccabee (*'Hurray!'*) won (*'Hurray!'*).

The Jewish people cleaned up the Temple in Jerusalem (*pointing East with the right hand*) and started to look for the special lamp (*cup hands*). At last they found it, but – oh dear! – there was only a tiny bit of oil left to put in the lamp (*cup hands*) and they had no time to make any more. The oil would only last for one day! So the Jewish people prayed to God and asked him to help. Then an amazing thing (*'Wow!'*) happened. The oil in the special lamp (*cup hands*) lasted not for one (*count on fingers*), or two, or three, or four, or five, or six, or seven days, but for eight whole days. What an amazing thing! (*'Wow!'*)

So at *Hanukkah* each year, Jewish people light candles every day to remember the time when the oil in the Temple burned for eight days.

(*At this point, the children could be shown how a hanukiah is lit. The candles can be left burning whilst they are given an opportunity to reflect on the story.*)

Reflection _____

Let us sit still for a moment and think about the story that we have just heard.

It is good to think about special times – times that have happened, and times that we can look forward to. Let's think quietly about them now – you might want to think about your birthday, or Christmas, or … (*add your own*).

Prayer _____

Dear God,
The story we have heard told of a wonderful thing that happened long ago, and how you look after those who keep your laws.
Thank you for helping us to remember special times in our lives, and we look forward to the special times that are to come.

Amen.

Suggestions for music

'Hanukkah holiday, festival of light' by Linda Swears (to sing)

Wish upon a star

Introduction

This assembly requires little preparation, and makes use of the wishes and desires of children – be prepared for some surprises; some children voice really heartfelt wishes. I have also used it like an advent calendar in December – one wish per day as the focus for our reflections.

Resources

- photocopies of star-shape – enough for each child to have one

If you are using wishes as an advent calendar, and if you have time, you may also need:

- coloured paper for mounting each star.

This has the advantage of making the stars last a little longer, too.

Timing

15–20 minutes for the assembly

About 5 minutes per day for the advent reflections

Preparation

Ask your class to think of something that they would really, really wish for. If you are doing this at Christmas time, it may be worth suggesting to the children that their wish should be for something other than a particular present. If they still have difficulty, try suggesting that their wish should be for someone else or something that cannot be bought in the shops. My own class suggested things like:

I wish that my grandad hadn't died
I wish that people would stop fighting
I wish it would snow this Christmas.

Once this sort of suggestion started coming, lots more followed.

Give each child a piece of star-shaped paper and ask them to write their wish, starting 'I wish that … .' If there is space, they could illustrate their wish, too.

If you intend to use the wishes as reflections for advent, write numbers 1 to 25 on the back of the stars. If you have more than 25 children in your class, the extra children could choose which day they would like to read their wish.

Pin the stars on a display board so that the numbers are showing, and muddled up.

The Advent reflections

As each day of Advent comes, the children find the star with the right number, then the child whose wish is on the back reads it out and explains it, if they want to. Then the wish can be pinned back on the board so that the writing can be seen. The weekend days can be read out on Mondays, and stars with dates in the Christmas holidays could be spread out over the last week of term, so that all the wishes have been read out before the end of term.

It's worth explaining about difficult wishes as they occur – most children in my class were able to distinguish between a wish that might come true and a wish that would be impossible (see the explanation in *Assembly,* below.)

The Assembly

(Welcome the children and explain that today we are going to be thinking about wishes. The children can read their wishes, and explain why they have wished it if they want to. Again, it's worth pausing between each child for a few seconds. Then continue.)

A wish is a wonderful thing – each of us carries lots of wishes and hopes inside of us. Every wish that you have heard is very real and very special to the child who has made it. They have all tried hard to think of wishes for other people or our world, to make things better.

Some people say that if you make a wish when you blow out candles on a birthday cake, or if you make a wish when you see a very bright star, it will come true. Some wishes, though, are very hard wishes; wishes that are difficult to grant – like bringing someone back to life, or changing something that has already happened.

Reflection

All of us have wishes inside us – it's part of being a human being, and it can make our world a better place when we work hard to make our wishes come true. People who believe in God may talk to him and tell him their wishes – it's called praying. Let's have a few quiet moments now to think about our own wishes.

Prayer

Dear God,
Thank you for listening to the wishes that we have inside. Help us always to wish for good things, that will make our world a better place to live in.

Amen.

(If you are using the Lord's Prayer music, explain that the words used in this song are a famous prayer called the Lord's Prayer which Jesus taught to his friends. You could then listen to the piece together before leaving the hall.)

Suggestions for music

'Nimrod' from *Enigma Variations* by Edward Elgar

'Lord's Prayer' from *African Sanctus* by David Fanshawe

'Wish upon a star' by Rose Royce

Christmas presents

Introduction

This is a rather more exciting way of retelling the Christmas story, and aims to help children to understand that for people who are Christians, it is the story of Jesus' birth that makes Christmas special. The assembly would work well if you were to read a version of the story, but it is even better if you are brave enough to tell it from memory.

Resources

- a nativity set – with separate pieces or pictures of each of the characters from the story. (To make the story work, you need at least Mary, Joseph, Baby Jesus, a shepherd and the wise men. If possible, also include an angel, a donkey, the manger, a sheep and a camel.)
- boxes of various sizes, one for each character used, one a lot larger than the others
- wrapping paper
- a gift tag for each character used
- the story of the nativity from a children's Bible. (A recommended version is listed in *Resources* on page 152.)

Timing

15–20 minutes

Preparation

Collect together the nativity pieces, or pictures (you could ask your class to draw them for you). Put the nativity pieces or pictures in the boxes. (Jesus should be in the largest one.) Then wrap them up, one at a time, in the same order as in the list below. If you are going to read the story, do not forget to check that the characters appear in the same order as listed. Attach a gift tag to each 'present', with a number on it for easy identification.

Mary
Angel*
Joseph
Donkey*

Manger*
Baby Jesus
Shepherd (and a sheep*)
Wise men (and their camel*)

(* *if you have one*)

Before the assembly starts, put the presents at the front of the hall, muddled up so that the children have to search for the box with the right number. It's very effective to put the presents under the school Christmas tree, if possible.

The Assembly

(Welcome the children and tell them that you are going to need some helpers for a very special job. Choose one helper for each present and explain that they are going to take it in turns to unwrap a present. Tell the first volunteer to find the present with number 1 on the label and ask them to unwrap it. The assembly can now proceed in one of two ways:

1 *Tell or read the appropriate part of the story as the child unwraps the parcel.*
   or
2 *Unwrap all the parcels – children could try to guess what might be in the next present – and then tell/read the whole story uninterrupted. Once the story is complete, continue.)*

Christmas is a very special and exciting time for lots of people – there are lots of things to get ready, presents to unwrap, food to eat, and people to visit.

Did you notice which character from the story was in the biggest box? *(Hopefully, the child who unwrapped the parcel should remember, even if the assembled children don't.)*

That's right, it was Baby Jesus.

Reflection

Let's have a few quiet moments to be still and think about what we have heard.

For people who are Christians, remembering the story of when Jesus was born is the biggest and the most special part of Christmas. They will enjoy all the lovely things about Christmas, but they will be thinking especially about Jesus being born in a stable in Bethlehem. Lots of them will go to church on Christmas Day to celebrate Jesus' birthday. For people who are Christians, Jesus is the biggest and best Christmas present of them all.

Prayer

Dear God,
Thank you for Christmas time, when we can have lots of exciting things to look forward to. As we remember the story of the special baby, Jesus, born in Bethlehem, we pray for peace throughout the world.

Amen.

Suggestions for music

A Christmas carol such as 'Away in a manger' or 'Silent Night' (to sing)

Getting ready

Introduction

This assembly is designed to introduce children to the idea of Lent – the period of 40 days before Easter when Christians remember Jesus' temptation in the desert. Many Christians give up something in remembrance that Jesus fasted for 40 days in the wilderness. Whilst this would not generally be the experience of the children in our schools, it is part of the Christian calendar that deserves a mention. The ideal day for this assembly would be Shrove Tuesday, which marks the day before Lent starts – if you're feeling brave, you could even cook (and toss) a pancake.

Resources

- a baby's rattle, bottle or toy
- a Christmas decoration
- a birthday cake candle
- a bottle of suntan cream
- a balloon
- a bowl containing a bag of flour, some eggs, some milk and a lemon
- cooking equipment for pancake making if you are intending to make pancakes
- a 'feelie' bag large enough to hold all the items above, excluding the ingredients and cooking equipment.

Timing

15 minutes (or more if you're making a pancake)

Preparation

Put all the objects (except the cooking ingredients) in the 'feelie' bag. Each object will represent an event that people get ready for, and will be discussed as it is chosen from the bag. Put the cooking ingredients out of sight until they are needed later in the assembly.

The Assembly

(Welcome the children and explain that today you are going to be thinking about how people get ready for different special occasions. Show them the 'feelie' bag and ask for some volunteers to come and pick something out. As each object is chosen, discuss it.

- *the baby's rattle, bottle or toy – Ask the children what this might be needed for and how someone might prepare for the arrival of a new baby*
- *the Christmas decoration – Ask the children what this reminds them of, and how people might get ready for Christmas*
- *the birthday cake candle – Ask the children what this is for, and how someone might need to prepare for a birthday*
- *the bottle of suntan cream – Ask the children when they might need this – hopefully, someone will suggest 'on holiday' – and how people might need to get ready to go away on holiday*
- *the balloon – Ask them what they think of when they see a balloon – 'parties' – and what people would have to do to get ready for a party. Then continue.)*

All these objects reminded us of special events that we need to get ready for – a new baby, Christmas, birthdays, holidays and parties. There are probably lots more. People who are Christians will soon be celebrating a special event – does anyone know what it is? (*If no one suggests Easter, then tell them.*) Easter is a really special time for Christians when they remember how Jesus died on a cross and was brought back to life again. Because it is so special to them, some Christians spend a long time getting ready – about 40 days, which is over a month. During those 40 days they think about how special Jesus is to them, and they might choose not to eat something that they really enjoy for those 40 days – things like chocolate, or biscuits or sweets. Now the day before they start giving up those chocolates or biscuits or sweets, they will have a bit of a celebration. That day is called 'Shrove Tuesday', although it does have another name which you might be able to guess after I've shown you what's in my bowl.

Does anyone know what delicious food you can make from flour and eggs and milk, something that you might put lemon juice on? (*Ask a few children for their suggestions – if the assembly is close to Shrove Tuesday, you stand a better chance of getting the correct answer.*) It's a pancake – and some of you might call Shrove Tuesday 'Pancake Day'.

Shrove Tuesday reminds Christians that it's time to get ready for Easter, time to remember that Jesus is special to them.

(At this point, you could make the pancake for everyone to see – but not eat, unless you're prepared to cook a few.)

Reflection

Let's have a few quiet moments to think about getting ready.

We are glad that there are so many things that we get ready for – for parties, holidays, Christmas and birthdays. It is exciting getting ready for these times because it reminds us that our special event is getting closer.

Prayer

Dear God,
We want to remember that now is a special time for people who are Christians, because they will be getting ready for Easter. We are glad that there are so many exciting things to get ready for, all the year round. It is exciting getting ready because it reminds us that our special event is getting closer.
Thank you, God, for these special times.

Amen.

Suggestions for music

'All in an Easter garden', traditional (to sing)

Easter egg-stravaganza!

Introduction

The credit for this assembly really goes to my class – the suggestions were all theirs! I wanted the assembly to focus on the theme of eggs as signs of new life, but didn't know where to start. I asked my children what they knew about eggs, and this assembly was the result. It needs very little preparation, and really made the other children think about what an amazing thing an egg is. We followed the assembly with an Easter egg hunt – a traditional children's game for Easter time – which made the connection between chocolate eggs and eggs as signs of new life.

Resources

- photocopies of the egg shape – one for each child in the class

If you are following the assembly with an Easter egg hunt:

- bags and bag ties
- enough mini-eggs for each child to have one, plus one each for their teachers and classroom assistants.

Timing

15–20 minutes, maybe a little longer for the egg hunt

Preparation

Ask your class to think of things that hatch out of eggs, and together make as long a list as you can (we came up with a list of at least 30 – from birds, through lizards, turtles and snakes to dinosaurs).

Each child needs to choose a different creature. Give them a blank egg and ask them to draw their creature clearly so that other children will be able to identify what their egg contains.

Discuss what we do with the eggs that we buy from the shops. Some children could draw these suggestions on some blank eggs. My class suggested fried, boiled, and scrambled eggs, or cakes, pancakes and omelettes.

If identification is difficult, write what the creature is inside the egg. Cut the eggs out carefully. Get each child to draw a crack on the back of their egg.

For the Easter egg hunt, place some eggs in plastic bags and tie them up. (How many eggs you put in each bag is up to you – I put enough for half a class in each bag, making two bags per class.) Before the assembly, hide the bags around the hall, or outside if you prefer and the weather is good. Leave a little of each bag showing so they are not too hard to find.

The Assembly

(Each child in your class will need to bring their egg, holding it so that the other children cannot see what is drawn on it, but so they can see the crack.

Welcome the children and explain that today we are going to be thinking about eggs and how amazing they are. Explain that each of the eggs that your class is holding has a different creature waiting to hatch out.

As each child tells the others what is inside their egg, they turn their egg around so that the drawing can be seen. It's worth pausing for a moment after each child has turned their egg around so that the children watching can take in what they are seeing.

When all the hatching eggs have been shown, the children put them down. Now the eggs showing all the ways to use eggs can be shown and explained. Then continue.)

Aren't eggs amazing? Think of all the different creatures in our world that hatch from eggs – birds, lizards, snakes, turtles, fish, tortoises, and even dinosaurs, before they all became extinct. In springtime, our world that has looked so dark and dead is coming back to life and lots of creatures are having babies. For some creatures, eggs are their way of having babies. From all these eggs come signs of new life. And some eggs can give us good things to eat – fried eggs, boiled eggs, scrambled eggs and all sorts of cakes.

Now at Easter time, what will you be looking forward to? (*Hopefully, a child will suggest chocolate Easter eggs.*)

That's right – Easter eggs! People give chocolate eggs at Easter time to remind each other of the new life that is all around us in the spring. People who are Christians, who believe in Jesus, give eggs to each other to remember the story from the Bible that tells of when Jesus died and came back to life again. (*Omit this reference to the story of Easter, if it is not one that is familiar to your children.*)

(*At this point, have some quiet moments for Reflection or for children to pray. Then, if you are following with the Easter egg hunt, go on to explain about the tradition, and choose two children from each class to hunt for the eggs.*

When the bags have been found, send the children with the eggs back to their own classes with instructions that each bag must be given to their teacher and shared so that each person in the class has an egg.)

Reflection

In our assembly today, we have been thinking about new life. How wonderful it is to see signs of new life all around us at Easter time, which is when Christians think about how Jesus died and came back to life again. Spring is a time for new leaves on the trees, flowers growing, lambs in the fields, eggs hatching. We are glad that the winter is over and that spring has come.

Prayer

Dear God,
Thank you for springtime and all the wonderful things that are happening in the world – all around us, we see signs of new life: new leaves on the trees, flowers growing, lambs in the fields, eggs hatching.
At Easter time as we are enjoying our Easter eggs, help us to remember the Easter story – that Jesus died and came back to life again.

Amen.

Suggestions for music

'This is the day' by Leslie Garrett (to sing)

'Spring' from *The Four Seasons* by Antonio Vivaldi

Easter music from Taizé, or Gregorian chants

'Hear the bells ringing' by Second Chapter of Acts

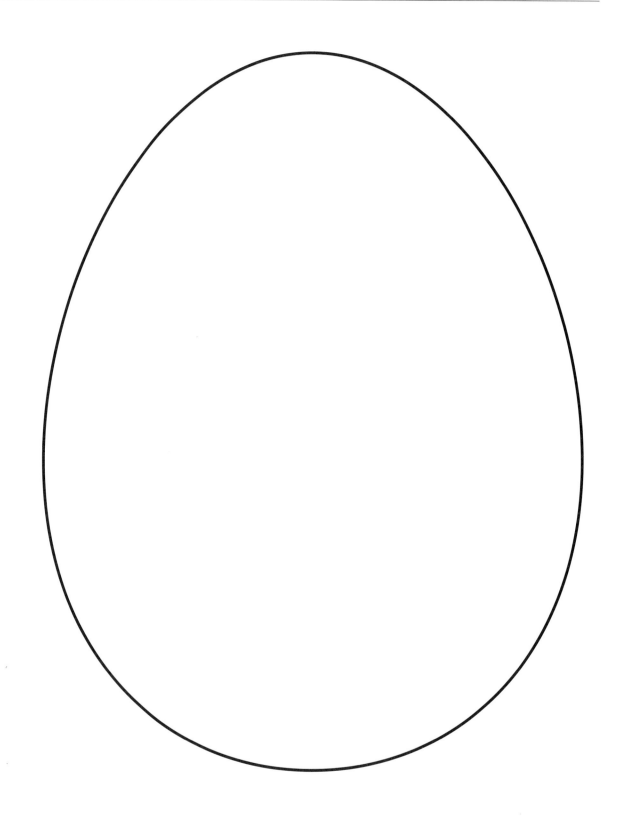

Who's your hero?

Introduction

Christian saints' days are quite often part of the school assembly calendar, but explaining to young children what a saint is can be quite a challenge! This quick assembly aims to do just that. In order for it to achieve its purpose, the assembly really needs to be presented on a saint's day – you could choose quite an obscure one since the focus is mainly on what a saint is, and does not go in any great depth into any particular saint. It requires a little advance preparation, and you will need an overhead projector – or alternatively some children dressed in their versions of super-hero costumes.

Resources

- an overhead projector
- OHP acetate
- a recording of one or more theme tunes to television 'super-hero' series – such as Superman, Batman etc. Alternatively, ask some children who have a range of super-hero costumes between them to bring their costumes in to dress up. Asking children to dress up is a good way of giving the children in the hall a clue as to who is coming next – not essential, but quite fun!

Timing

10–15 minutes

Preparation

Onto OHP acetate, draw a selection of super-hero symbols (i.e. what they usually have emblazoned across their super-hero costumes, such as the Superman 'S', Spiderman's web or the Batman symbol). You will need to draw them in such a way that you can uncover them on the OHP one at a time. (Sporting heroes could be included, too.)

You could use a combination of costumes and symbols, to cover a wider range. If you are planning to use children, you will need to create a place where they can remain hidden until their moment comes.

You will also need to do a little research into the saint's day that you are going to be conducting this assembly on – a book called *Red Letter Days* (listed in *Resources* on page 151) is very useful for this purpose.

The Assembly

(Welcome the children and explain that today we are going to be thinking about some special people called heroes. Ask if any of the children present can explain what a hero is. Then continue.)

A hero can be someone who does brave things to save people who are in danger, or it can be someone who you really want to be like when you grow up. Many of you will know some characters who are heroes – let's see if you can guess these heroes' names.

(Go on to the guessing game – uncover the OHP symbols that you have drawn on the acetate, one at a time, and ask children to identify the super-hero from the symbol, or use the theme tunes, or ask your children dressed in costumes to show themselves, one at a time, for others to identify. Talk briefly about why each is a hero, focusing especially on their good deeds.

This activity will probably cause a fair bit of excitement, so wait until the children have settled, then continue. If there are any children wearing Rainbows, Brownies, Beavers or Cubs uniforms, as sometimes is the custom in schools on saints' days, ask them if they know why they are wearing them today.)

Today is St _____ Day. The word 'saint' is quite difficult to explain, which is why we thought first about heroes. To people who are Christians, saints are a bit like heroes. Saints are people who have lived very good lives, or sometimes were even killed just for believing in God. Christians want to live good lives that please God, just like the saints did. Thinking about the lives of the saints can help them to try harder. That's why there are saints' days, when Christians remember these special people and are reminded to try to live good lives themselves.

(At this point, you will need to explain a little about the saint's day that you are remembering – these are just a few possibilities:

30 November – St Andrew	*10 December – St Nicholas*
1 February – St Brigid	*1 March – St David*
17 March – St Patrick	*23 April – St George*
25 April – St Mark	*29 June – St Peter*
25 July – St Christopher or St James	*4 October – St Francis)*

Reflection

Let us sit quietly for a moment and think about our own heroes, people we admire. We have been thinking today about St _____ who is remembered for being ... (list some of the good qualities that are linked with this saint). As we go through today, may we try to live our lives in ways that are helpful to others – by being kind, or generous, or putting someone else first.

Prayer

Dear God,
We have been thinking about the good life that St _____ lived.
As we go through today, help us to live our lives in ways that are helpful to others – by being kind, or generous, or putting someone else first.

Amen.

Suggestions for music

'Holding out for a hero' by Bonnie Tyler

'Hero' by Mariah Carey

Bravery

Introduction

This is a very quick assembly to prepare for. It is designed to help children to understand why people remember St George's Day.

Resources

- OHP
- photocopiable acetate
- red permanent marker
- OHP pens (water-soluble, so that you can re-use the acetate at a later date)
- photocopy of shield shape.

Timing

15 minutes

Preparation

Photocopy the shield onto photocopiable acetate. Colour the cross in the centre red, using the permanent marker. This shield will be used for your reflection or prayer – the empty sections will be filled with children's suggestions about times when we can be brave.

The Assembly

(Welcome the children and introduce the story.)

This is the story that people remember on St George's Day – 23 April – every year. Saints are special people – people who have lived very good lives. Many people who are Christians will try to live good lives like the saints did. This is the story of St George and the dragon … .

The story of St George and the dragon

Long, long ago there lived a king who had a very beautiful daughter whom he loved very much. This king ruled over a small town, and he took good care of the people who lived there. For many years they all lived happily.

Then one terrible day, a huge dragon came to the town and started attacking the people who lived there. It had a tail longer than a house, huge, scaly wings that blocked out the sun when it flapped them, and teeth like swords. To start with, the dragon was content just to frighten the people by roaring, or burning down their houses with its fiery breath. The king sent out his soldiers, but they could do nothing to stop the dragon – their swords were just not strong enough weapons against the enormous, scaly beast. But then it got hungry. The next day, the dragon demanded that the king should send him a nice, juicy person to eat. The king sent out his brave knights in their shining armour, but their spears only scratched the dragon's thick skin. So he wrote one name at a time on lots of small pieces of paper, until the name of every person who lived in the town was written down. Then he put all the names in a bag, and took one out. The person whose name was written on that piece of paper would be the dragon's breakfast.

Days went by, and the dragon still demanded more and more people. Then one dreadful day, when the dragon demanded his supper, the king drew out the name of his beautiful daughter, the princess. Sadly, he watched as she walked down the hillside to where the dragon was living.

That same day, a new knight had ridden into the town on his beautiful white horse. Every knight had a shield to protect him when he went into battle. This knight carried a shield with a cross on it – a sign that he loved God. He would often ask God to help him in the dangerous situations that he faced. He was brave and bold, and when he heard about what had been happening in the town, he decided that he must try to end the suffering of the people and kill this terrible creature. He prayed to God, and asked him for help in the fight against the dragon. Then he rode to the cave where it lived. The dragon heard him coming and came out to see what he had been brought for his breakfast. There was a battle, but finally the knight was victorious – the dragon was dead!

The knight's name was George, and his bravery is remembered by many people on St George's Day each year.

This is what St George's shield looked like. (*Turn on the OHP.*) Can you see the cross?

We have been thinking today about St George's bravery. Can you think of any times when you have been very brave?

(Ask children to make suggestions – they are usually only too willing! As they make suggestions, write them onto the shield in the parts that are not coloured. Each phrase will need to start with the words 'When we...', as these phrases will make up your reflection prayer. There is probably room for about eight suggestions – two in each section.)

Reflection

Now let's have a few quiet moments while we think or pray. I am going to read out the suggestions you have given me, and at the end of each one I shall say 'Help us to be brave'. If you would like to, please join in with me.

Prayer

Dear God,
When we ... help us to be brave.

Amen.

Suggestions for music

'Mars – Bringer of War' from *The Planets* by Gustav Holst

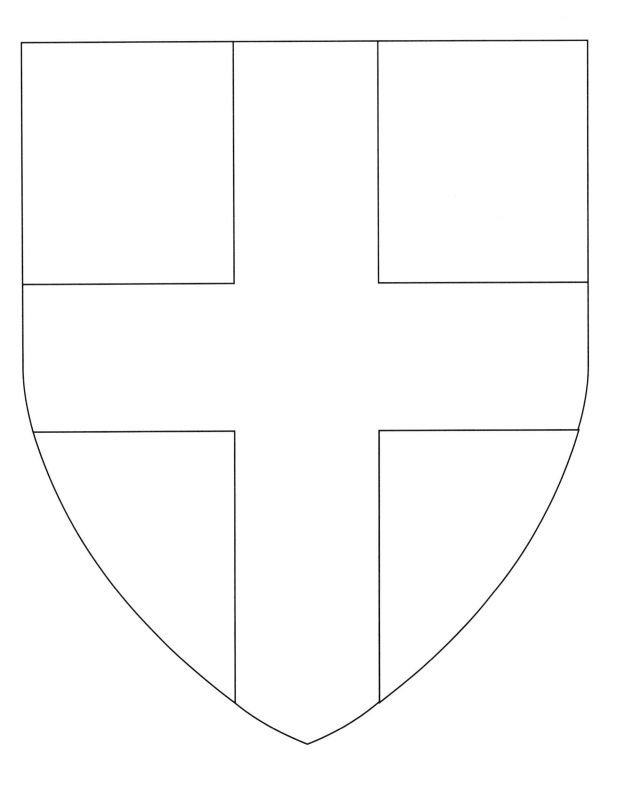

Just around the corner!

Introduction

This assembly was written for and performed by a class of four and five-year-olds. It is designed to help children to think about some of the beautiful things that happen around springtime. It needs a little rehearsal since a small group of children act out the story. It is designed to be a shorter assembly, but could easily be lengthened by adding extra elements which you feel are appropriate.

Resources

- some signs of spring e.g. catkin tails, pussy willow buds, spring flowers, frog spawn, new leaves on trees etc. – you could add in as many as you like!
- a tape recording of birdsong (such as those which accompany listening lotto games, where the sounds of different animals have to be identified)
- some screens or stage blocks to create corners for children to look around.

Timing

10 minutes

Preparation

Gather as many signs of spring as you require for the story.

Before the assembly, choose as many children (or pairs of children if preferred) to act out the story as you have signs of spring. They will need to have a strong leader who will be able to remember where to lead the group next! In this story, three signs of spring are found. If you want to include more, you could add more.

At the front of the hall, set up some stage blocks or screens and hide the signs of spring behind them so that they cannot be seen from the front. The blocks also create corners for the story.

Rehearse the story with the small group of children that you have chosen. The leader will need to lead them on a journey between the two stage blocks or screens and the children will, in turn, need to collect a sign of spring as they find it 'around the corner'. The whole class can join in with the parts where it says '_____ class said'. You will need to add in your name and your class' name. As each spring item is found, you may want to talk about it with the children gathered in assembly.

The Assembly

(Welcome the children and ask them if they know which season we are in at the moment – almost certainly, someone will suggest spring! Explain that lots of really wonderful things happen in the springtime, and that today's assembly is going to help them to think about some of them. Then continue with the story. The group of children will need to follow the instructions as you read them.)

_____ class goes looking for spring

One day, I said, 'This is a cold, grey day, but spring is just around the corner.'

_____ class wanted spring to come, so they went out for a walk to see if they could find spring on the other side of the corner.

_____ class went out of the classroom and around the corner (*first stage block*) to see if spring was on the other side.

I asked, 'Have we found it?'

_____ class said, ' Yes!' (*The first child collects their sign of spring from behind the first corner. Discuss it if desired.*)

_____ class went on a bit further and found another corner (*second stage block*). They went around the corner to see if spring was on the other side.

I asked, 'Have we found it?'

_____ class said, 'Yes!' (*The second child collects their sign of spring from behind the second corner. Discuss if desired.*)

_____ class found one more corner (*back to first stage block again*). They went around it to see if spring was on the other side.

I asked, 'Have we found it?'

But _____ class said, 'No, we can't see anything.'

So I said, 'Close your eyes and listen.' (*Encourage everyone to close their eyes, then play the tape of the birdsong.*)

'We love springtime,' said _____ class. 'So do I,' I said.

Reflection

In the story, the children found just a few beautiful things that are signs that spring is here – there are lots more. I expect you could think of some. Let's have a few moments of quiet to think about how beautiful our world is in the spring.

Prayer

Dear God,

Thank you for this lovely time of year when our cold, grey world begins to come to life again.

Thank you for beautiful spring flowers, for new green leaves, for warm sunshine and the sound of birdsong which fills the air.

Amen.

Suggestions for music

'Spring' from *The Four Seasons* by Antonio Vivaldi

'On hearing the first cuckoo in Spring' by Delius

All the same, but different

Introduction

This assembly would link quite well with 'Beautiful inside' (see page 41). It is an adaptation of an African myth, and tries to answer the question, 'Why do we have skin of different colours?' It emphasizes the fact that although our skin colours may be different, we are all human beings. It's a useful story to tell if there have been problems of a racial nature at school.

Timing

10–15 minutes

The Assembly

(Welcome the children.)

Some of you might have wondered why there are so many different shades of skin colour. A long time ago, people would often tell stories to help explain things that were difficult to understand. The story we are going to hear today is a very old African story, and was probably told to try to explain why there are people with skins of so many different colours.

The story of the fire children

Nyame, the sky-god, lived alone in space above the darkness of the African night sky. One day, he decided to take a basket of earth and fill it with all kinds of living things – animals, insects, birds and plants. He hung it in the sky, and it became the Earth. Because he wanted to be able to visit the Earth from time to time, he made a trapdoor in the sky so that he could climb down onto the Earth. He also made little holes in the sky so that when the trapdoor was closed, the Earth would not be left in darkness. The trapdoor and the holes are the moon and the stars.

One day, he looked down through his trapdoor and saw that part of the Earth had become bare, so he filled another basket with plants and growing things and lowered it on a rainbow rope down through the trapdoor.

Inside Nyame lived some spirit-people, and two of them decided they would climb up inside him to look out through his mouth to see what he was doing. But Nyame sneezed just as they reached his mouth, and blew them out through the trapdoor. They fell down through the sky, and onto the Earth. What a strange and beautiful place the Earth was, full of colourful plants and strange animals. They found a cave to live in, and settled down to their new life – after all, how would they get back up through the trapdoor?

Often, the woman-spirit, whose name was Iyaloda, was left alone in the cave when the man-spirit went off to explore, and she used to get very lonely. One day, she thought of a way to end her loneliness at last, and told the man-spirit her plan.

He wasn't pleased when she told him. 'What do you mean, you've made a plan? The last plan you made ended up with us being left stranded here on Earth – I knew that I shouldn't have listened to you when you said it would be safe for us to look out through Nyame's mouth!'

But Iyaloda begged him to listen to her and began to explain.

'Let's make some small creatures from clay, and shape them like ourselves,' she said. 'We can make a fire, bake them and breathe life into them so that they can walk around like us. Then when you go off into the forest, they'll be able to keep me company, and I won't be lonely any more. We could call them children.'

She waited to see what he would say about her plan. He was quite relieved that the plan seemed so simple, and said that they should try it out. So the next day, they built up the fire until it glowed red hot, and carefully made little figures from the clay that Iyaloda dug up from the ground outside the cave. They put the tiny models into the fire to bake, and waited.

Just then, they heard the great footsteps of Nyame as he crashed through the forest, and they heard him calling out their names. They were terrified because they didn't want to be discovered doing anything that might make Nyame angry, so they snatched the little clay people out of the fire and wrapped them in leaves to hide them.

They were just hiding the last figure when Nyame appeared at the entrance to the cave and stood looking at them. 'Well,' he said, 'how do you like the Earth? And have you been behaving yourselves?'

'Oh, yes,' they replied, bowing before him. 'Well, see that you continue to be good, and take care of this Earth that I made,' he boomed. And away he went, into the forest. As soon as he had gone, they set about making a new batch of little clay people and put them into the fire. No sooner had they done so, than Nyame appeared again. This time they hadn't a chance to get the little clay people out of the fire and hide them, so they had to leave them in the fire and hope that Nyame wouldn't notice. He stayed longer this time, and seemed to be a little suspicious, but he eventually left and their secret was safe. Nyame visited several more times before he returned to the sky. Sometimes they would hear him coming, and be able to take the little clay people out of the fire and hide them before he got to the cave. Other times, they would have to leave them baking in the fire until he had gone.

When Nyame had left to go back to the sky, the spirit-people were able to take all the clay children from their hiding places and look at what they had made. Some of the little clay people had been in the fire such a short time that they were hardly baked at all and quite white in colour. Others were yellow, some red or brown, and still others were baked until they had burned quite black.

The spirit-people were really pleased with what they had made, no matter what colour they were. They breathed their breath into each clay figure, and the tiny people came to life. Iyaloda would be lonely no more.

Reflection

Let's share some quiet moments now, to reflect on what we have been thinking about today.

In the story, there were little people whose skin colours were all different shades, just like there are in our world today. It doesn't matter what colour our skin is, we are all human beings living on the same Earth. Some people have darker skin because they live in countries where the sun is stronger, or because they spend more time out in the sun than other people do. Others have paler skin because they live in countries where it is cooler and the rays of the sun are not so strong. We all belong to the human race – whatever the colour of our skin.

There are many ways that we are different from each other – the colour of our eyes, our hair and our skin. Each one of us is unique and special. But may we always remember that underneath we are all human beings.

Prayer

Dear God,
You have made each one of us different from anyone else – each one of us is
unique and special. The colours of our eyes, skin or hair may be different, but
you made us all human beings. Thank you.

Amen.

Suggestions for music

'Ebony and Ivory' by Paul McCartney and Stevie Wonder

Save our world!

Introduction

This assembly is similar in concept to 'How to mend a broken heart' (see page 7), but back-to-front! It requires a little more preparation, and some artwork or pictures. The issue of conservation is one close to the hearts of many of our children and this assembly encourages them to think about some of the ways that we have not looked after our world and to reflect on how to make things better.

Resources

- an outline map of the world
- A3 card – photocopying onto blue card saves time colouring in the sea
- pictures of the following, cut from magazines, or drawn by you or the children, or even pictures from books:
  a fox, a bird's nest, litter, pollution, tree-cutting in a rainforest, an elephant.

Timing

20 minutes

Preparation

Copy the world outline onto A3 blue card, then colour the land parts green.

If you are using the assembly as a follow-up to the creation story, write around the outside edge of the outline 'God said, "Take care of my beautiful world."' Omit this section if you are not referring to creation. If necessary, trim the sides of the card to remove any excess from the outside of the outline.

Prepare the pictures to represent various aspects of humankind's handling of the world. (More detailed explanations are to be found in the *Assembly* notes.) Then cut the world picture into as many pieces as you have pictures – remember not to cut the pieces too small, and make each a little different in shape to make it easier to put the puzzle back together again. (Write numbers on the reverse in pencil too if you wish.)

The notes in the *Assembly* section are, as near as possible, the mental notes I made for myself. Assemblies often work better if I have used my own way of explaining things, rather than reading from a piece of paper. You may prefer to make your own notes.

Before the assembly starts, put the world puzzle together, on the board or wall, using Blutac, so that the world looks complete and the text is clearly visible.

The Assembly

Welcome the children and, if using this as a follow-up to an assembly on the story of creation, ask the children if they can remember what the theme of the last assembly was.

Then explain that Christians – also Jews and Muslims – believe that God gave his world to humankind – human beings – to look after. Continue by looking at the outline of the world and reading the text that is written around it, explaining it as you feel appropriate.

Then explain that you have a 'backwards-puzzle' to help them to decide how well human beings have looked after our world.

Show the pictures one at a time, asking one child each time to say what they can see. Then discuss the picture with the children.

- *fox – hunting animals for sport*
- *bird's nest – illegally stealing animals (in this case, bird's eggs) for private collections*
- *litter or pollution – rubbish and pollution dumped in our rivers and oceans can kill animals and destroy their habitat*
- *cutting down rainforests – the uses we have for timber felled in rainforests is perfectly acceptable (paper, building, fuel, clearing land for crops and homes), but the problem is that large areas are cleared, leaving many creatures homeless; often, no new saplings are planted to replace the homes that creatures have lost.*
- *elephant – killing animals because of our desire to be beautiful (tusks for ornaments, jewellery etc., animal skins for coats etc.).*

As you finish discussing each picture, ask the child you chose initially to pick a piece of jigsaw puzzle and remove it from the board. By the end of the discussion time, the world should – literally – have been taken to pieces in front of the children's eyes.

Explain to the children that people are destroying our world, breaking it up, when they do all those things that have been seen in the pictures. Have we taken care of our world?

This is quite a negative way to end an assembly, so it is important at this point to ask children to consider what we as human beings could do to improve or change what is being done to our world – they often have much clearer ideas than adults do! Encourage them to think of ways in which they, personally, can help, such as picking up litter left in the playground, or recycling bottles and cans etc.

As they suggest ways, build the world up in front of them until it is complete – this got a spontaneous round of applause when I did it, so be prepared!

Reflection

We have been thinking today of the ways that people have harmed our beautiful world. As we grow up, may we find ways of showing that we care about the world that we live in.

Prayer

Dear God,
We are sorry that we have not taken very good care of your beautiful world – we know it makes you sad.
Please help us to find ways of showing that we do care about the world that we live in, so that we can grow up in a world that is still beautiful.

Amen.

Suggestions for music

'What a wonderful world' by Louis Armstrong

Waste not, want not!

Introduction

Water is a precious resource and is vital for living, but it is one of many things that we generally take for granted, until we find ourselves without it. This assembly is designed to make children more aware of how much we rely on there always being water in our taps. The assembly requires a little preparation in advance – by your class once again!

Resources

- information about the use of water prepared by you and your class.

Timing

15–20 minutes, depending on how many children's mimes you use

Preparation

A few days before the assembly, tell your class that you want them to think about water, and when we use it.

Ask them to tell you every time they use water for something at school, and make a note of what they say, somewhere the whole class can see. You might need to make some suggestions – such as washing hands, flushing the toilet, mixing paint, drinking at playtime etc. It does not matter if someone else has already made a particular suggestion; what is important is that the children are noticing that they have used water.

Then ask the children to carry on noticing when water is used while they are at home so that they can tell everyone else the next day – see how many suggestions they can come up with, and challenge them to be clever. Add these to the list as they tell you. If they have forgotten to notice, you may have to use a few probing questions such as, 'Did anyone's mum or dad make a cup of tea?' or, 'Did anyone clean their teeth last night?' Don't forget that water is used in cooking as well!

Now you need to practise the game that you will play in assembly. Ask the children to think of one way that they have used water, and play-act it in front of the other children. Can you guess what they are doing? These mimes will form the introduction to your assembly – so make a note of the best ones and allow the children to practise.

The Assembly

(Welcome the children and explain that today's assembly is going to be all about something that we use so often that we don't even think about it. Tell them that some of your children are going to do some mimes and ask the assembled children to try to guess what they are doing. Start with the really obvious ones so that they quickly get the idea. Ask the children to repeat them if necessary.

When they have all finished, tell them that all the children were using the same thing. Can anyone tell you what it was? Hopefully, they will tell you it was water! Then continue.)

Water is something that we all use, every day. Think for a moment of all the things that my children were using water for. (*List some.*)

What would life be like if one day, when we turned on the taps, there was no water? We wouldn't be able to clean our teeth, or make a cup of tea, or have a wash, a bath or a shower. We wouldn't be able to water our plants and they would all shrivel up and die. We wouldn't be able to flush the toilet, or wash our hands, or make orange squash. We wouldn't be able to wash our clothes, and all our plates and bowls would stay dirty. Our lives would be quite different. What would happen if somebody, somewhere was so greedy that they used up all our water?

There is an old Australian folk tale about an enormous, greedy frog called Tiddalik. This story might have been told to warn people not to be greedy with their water.

The story of Tiddalik

One hot, sunny day, Tiddalik decided that he needed a drink of water to cool him down. So he went down to the lake for a drink. Lots of other animals were already there – there was Kangaroo, and Wombat, and Koala, and Snake, all drinking from the lake. Tiddalik saw them drinking, and decided that he didn't want to share the water in the lake with anyone. So he swallowed all the water, in one great, big gulp – no more lake, and no more water for the animals.

Time went by and the sun got hotter and hotter. The other animals in the forest got more and more thirsty, until they could bear it no more. So they called a meeting and decided that something must be done to make Tiddalik give them back their water. 'We must make him open his mouth,' said Kangaroo.

'Let's make him laugh,' suggested Koala. So off they went to find Tiddalik and put their plan into action.

Tiddalik was still sitting by the edge of the lake, so full of water that he could hardly move. One by one, the animals tried to make Tiddalik laugh – they pulled funny faces and told funny jokes. They turned somersaults and pretended to fall over one another like clowns, but nothing seemed to work.

They were near to giving up when Wombat had a really good idea. He sneaked up behind Tiddalik and, ever so gently to begin with, he started to tickle him. Tiddalik began to tremble, but his mouth stayed shut tight. So Wombat tickled some more – the corners of Tiddalik's mouth began to twitch. Some more tickling, and Tiddalik could not keep his mouth closed a second longer. He let out an enormous giggle and out flowed all the water, back into the lake where it belonged – enough water for everyone to share.

Reflection

Now that was just a story, but there is a lesson we can learn from it. We all have water to share, but we need to be careful not to be greedy like Tiddalik, or waste it. That's why there are times, if the summer is very hot and dry, when we are told not to use lots of water on our gardens, or we are told not to leave taps running. If we are not careful, and we waste our precious water, we might just find one day that we turn on our taps and no water comes out.

Let's have a few quiet moments to think now.

When we clean our teeth, when we have a drink, when we wash our hands or when we have a bath, may we remember that water is precious – we all need water.

Prayer

Dear God,
We are grateful that we always have water in our taps. Thank you for sending the rain which gives us water for all our needs. Next time we turn on a tap, help us to use water wisely and not be wasteful.

Amen.

Suggestions for music

'La Mer' by Claude Debussy

Water of life

Introduction

This assembly is designed to link with 'Waste not, want not!' (see page 99). It is aimed at making children more aware of how fortunate we are to have clean water to drink, when there are many people in our world for whom clean water is a luxury. Very little preparation is necessary.

Resources

- a large glass and a spoon
- small amounts of:
  sand and fine soil
  washing powder
  shower gel
- pictures of water usage in the Developing World, e.g. people washing clothes in the river etc. (TEAR Fund is a good source of OHP transparencies and posters.)

Timing

10–15 minutes

Preparation

Fill a large glass with water. Put the glass on a table at the front of the hall, for all to see. Collect the substances to put into the water.

The Assembly

(Welcome the children to the assembly. Then continue.)

I expect all of you could tell me what I have on the table in front of me, but I wonder if anyone can tell me where this glass of water came from?

(Ask a child to answer the question – hopefully, they will say that it came from the tap.)

That's right, I turned on the tap and out the water came, ready for me to drink. *(Invite a child to come and take a sip of water from the glass.)*

Does anybody know where the water in our taps comes from? (*Invite a few children to respond, and congratulate them if they can tell you.*)

When it rains, the water collects in big lakes called reservoirs. The water then goes through lots of pipes into a waterworks that cleans the water and makes it safe for us to drink. Then the water travels through lots more pipes into our homes. So when we turn on the tap, out comes clean, safe water.

It is very easy for us to forget that there are many people in our world who can't just turn on a tap in their home when they want some water – or put on the washing machine when their clothes are dirty. Lots of people in countries like India or Africa (*Use photographs if you have them.*) don't have taps to turn on – if they want water, they have to walk to the nearest river or lake.

This water that they drink comes straight from the river or lake, so it will probably have sand and dirt in it. Let's add some to my glass of water and see what happens. (*Add the sand and dirt to the water and give it a stir. Hold the glass up for everyone to see.*) Would you like to drink it now?

The water might also have been used by other people to wash their clothes, even though it doesn't look very clean – imagine drinking water from the washing machine! (*Add the washing powder to the glass and stir.*) People in the Developing World probably wouldn't use washing powder like we do, but the water would still not be very nice to drink would it? Would you like to have a drink from the glass now?

The people would probably have used the same water to wash themselves – would you like to drink the water after you'd taken a bath in it? Let's add a little soap to the water and see how it looks. (*Add the shower gel and stir.*) Now who'd like to drink this water?

The water would have had animals drinking from it, or walking through it too – everybody uses the water from the rivers and lakes because that's all there is to use.

The water in the lakes and rivers is used for everything – washing, drinking and cooking. Imagine what it would be like if the only water you had to drink was water like this. (*Hold up the glass.*) Yuk! Some people may have to walk long distances to lakes or rivers to fetch water to use, and sometimes if it has been very hot and dry, there may be little or no water when they get there.

We have probably all seen pictures on the news, or programmes like *Blue Peter,* of people who live in poorer countries. Many of them may have become ill just because they drank water that was not clean. Without clean water, they may even die. Fortunately, there are people in our world who will go to these countries and help the people who live there to build machinery to clean the water. There are still many places where there is no clean, safe water.

Reflection

We are so lucky that we can just turn on the tap in the kitchen to get a nice, cool drink of clean, fresh water, or turn on the taps in the bathroom to have a lovely, warm bath or shower. We have toilets that flush, and clean water for cleaning our teeth. We hardly ever have to worry that there will be no water in the taps when we turn them on. Let's have a few quiet moments to think about how fortunate we are.

When we have a drink, or wash our clothes, or have a bath, may we be grateful that we have clean water. May we also spare a thought for people in other countries who are not yet able to have safe, clean water.

Prayer

Dear God,
We are sad that, in poorer countries, many people die because they have no clean water to drink.
Thank you for the people who are willing to go to these places and help to make the water safe to drink. When we turn on our taps, please help us to remember how fortunate we are.

Amen.

Suggestions for music

'Orinoco Flow' from *Watermark* by Enya

'The Aquarium' from *Carnival of the Animals* by Saint Saëns

We are all special

Introduction

This assembly is based on a retelling of the story of The Lost Sheep. It requires a little preparation in advance, and does tend to make for a rather lively assembly. The children get very involved.

Resources

- an overhead projector
- nine copies of the ten-sheep sheet – on photocopiable OHP acetate if possible, but it will also work if the sheep are photocopied onto ordinary paper
- one copy of the nine-sheep sheet – again on OHP acetate or paper
- one cuddly lamb or sheep – borrowed from a child if you don't have one
- ten envelopes large enough to put an OHP acetate sheet inside.

Timing

20 minutes

Preparation

Photocopy the sheep sheets as directed in the *Resources* above, and put each one inside an envelope. Make sure that you know which is the envelope with the nine sheep inside, perhaps you could put a mark on it to distinguish it from the others.

Ask a member of staff (or a very sensible child), who you think wouldn't mind, to be prepared to bleat like a sheep at the appropriate point in the story. They must be able to do this quite surreptitiously, so that it is quite hard for both the shepherd and the children in the hall to locate the 'lost sheep'. Explain to them the cue in the story when they are needed, and rehearse if necessary. When I did this assembly, we used a tape recording of a sheep which a member of staff turned on and off just outside the hall door – the children were absolutely convinced that there was a real sheep in the hall!

Before the assembly, 'hide' the nine envelopes with ten sheep inside around the hall so that they can be seen relatively easily. Make the envelope with the nine sheep inside more difficult to find. Also, give the mystery 'bleater' the cuddly lamb to keep hidden, until the appropriate moment.

Select one child to be the shepherd – choose someone who can count to ten reliably.

The Assembly

(At the start of this assembly, welcome the children and explain to them that this is a rather exciting story and that you will need their help to make it work well.)

This is a story from the Christian Bible. Jesus told it to his special friends to help them to understand how much God loved them and that although there are many people in the world, each one of them is really special to God.

The story of the lost sheep

Once there lived a shepherd *(Shepherd stands up.)* who had lots and lots of sheep. One hundred sheep in fact. He was a very good shepherd and he took great care of all his sheep. He would lead them to the best, green grass and find them the deepest, clearest streams to drink from. He cared so much for his sheep that he gave them all names, and he knew the sound of each sheep's voice. Every night before it got dark, he would round them all up and count them, to make sure he had them all before he put them safely in the sheepfold for the night. One night, he began to count his sheep. This is how he did it:

(Explain that the sheep are in envelopes all around the room. The shepherd needs to 'round up' all the envelopes that they can see and bring the sheep to be counted. Make sure that all the envelopes have been found and put the marked envelope on the bottom of the pile. Open each envelope one at a time and put each sheet on the OHP – or hold the paper up – for the shepherd to count. Other children in the hall could also be used to help the shepherd to count – it keeps their interest. As each sheet is counted, add it to the running total, until 99 sheep have been counted.)

How many sheep was that? Let's count those last few again to make sure we haven't made a mistake. Only 99! Which one is missing? It's Lambkin, a small lamb who's only a few weeks old. Where could he be? What shall we do? *(Ask for suggestions – hopefully, someone will suggest that the shepherd goes to look for the lost sheep!)*

So the shepherd went out into the fields to look for his lost sheep.

(Send the shepherd to 'search' the room. Allow the shepherd to search for a while. Wait until the shepherd is a distance away from the hidden Lambkin before saying the cue for the 'bleater' to bleat softly.)

But wait! Was that a sound? (*'Bleater' bleats softly.*)

The shepherd stopped still, to listen more carefully. (*More bleats.*) Yes! He was sure that he had heard a sheep bleating. Now all he had to do was follow the sound to find his lost sheep. (*The shepherd 'searches' and eventually locates the 'bleater' with the sheep.*)

Hurray! The shepherd carried Lambkin back cradled in his arms, glad that his lost sheep was safe at last.

Reflection

Let's have a few moments to be quiet and think about the story we have just heard. The shepherd had lots and lots of sheep, just as there are lots and lots of people in the world. The shepherd was really concerned about that one lost sheep because every last one of his sheep was really special to him. It says in the Bible that even though there are millions of people in the world, every single person in the world is special to God.

When we are feeling lonely, lost or unloved, this story can remind us that we are all special – to each other, to our teachers, to our mums and dads, to all our families. Each one of us is loved by somebody.

Prayer

Dear God,
Thank you that this story reminds us of how special we are and that you love each one of us very much. When we are feeling lost or lonely, help us to remember that we are special and loved.

Amen.

Suggestions for music

Excerpts from *Symphony no. 6 'Pastoral'* by Beethoven

'Don't give up' by Peter Gabriel

Every little helps!

Introduction

This assembly needs very little preparation. It makes use of a child's lunch, so you just need to remember to ask a child if you can borrow their lunch box before you go into assembly – they will get it back intact! The story is a retelling of one of Jesus' miracles – the feeding of the 5000.

Resources

- a child and their lunch box – containing food. (It's worth reassuring the child whose lunch you borrow that they will get it all back, and tell the other children that they will not be keeping any of the food!)

Timing

15–20 minutes

The Assembly

(Welcome the children, and explain that someone in your class has brought their lunch to show you all. Then continue.)

You're probably all wondering why I've asked _____ to bring his/her lunch box into assembly. No – it's not because I'm feeling hungry, or that I've forgotten what time lunch time is! I'm hoping that this lunch will help me to tell you a story.

Now, let's have a look at what's inside. *(Talk the children through the contents, and show them.)*

How many children do you think could share this lunch?

(Pretend to share the lunch amongst the other children – 'You can have the crisps', etc.)

Do you think they'd be full when they'd finished? What if we tried to share the lunch with everyone in the hall – would they all get some, do you think? Some of you might be lucky enough to get a whole crisp, or a nibble of a sandwich, or maybe even a tiny sip of the drink. Would we all have full tummies? I expect we would all be rather hungry if that's all we had to eat for our lunch.

Today's story is from the Bible. It's all about a little boy and how he shared his packed lunch.

The story of the boy who shared his lunch

Wherever Jesus went, you could usually be sure that there would be crowds of people with him, for people loved to listen to his stories. They would come from miles around to hear what he had to say to them. One beautiful, sunny day a crowd of about 5000 had followed Jesus to the hillside – what a lot of people! That's about seventeen halls full of children. (*Change this to suit the numbers you have.*) Jesus sat them down on the grass and began to talk to them. Many people had come to listen to Jesus' stories. Others had come because they were sick and wanted Jesus to make them better. Jesus loved to help people, and felt sad that many of them were ill, so he touched them and they became well again.

The day passed and evening came, and still there were lots of people sitting on the hillside, by the sea called Galilee, listening to Jesus. Some of them were beginning to grumble, because they were hungry. Just imagine the noise of 5000 rumbling tummies! Jesus' special friends heard what some of the people were saying, and they went to Jesus and said, 'It's getting late and the people are hungry. Let's send them into the villages to buy some food.' But Jesus told his friends to find the people some food. Where could they go to buy enough food for 5000 people? It would cost an absolute fortune! And even if they had the money, it would take such a long time to carry it all back from the villages. Jesus couldn't really mean it, could he?

Now, amongst all these people, there was a little boy. He'd gone to the lake to do a bit of fishing, and he hadn't expected all these people to be there as well. All their chattering had frightened the fish away, but he didn't mind too much because he'd had a chance to hear Jesus' stories for himself. As usual, his mum had given him some lunch to eat – five little bread rolls, and two small fish. He heard Jesus' friends talking and moaning to each other. He went to one of the friends, whose name was Andrew, and said, 'I don't know if this is any help, but here's my packed lunch.' Imagine Andrew's face – just five bread rolls and two fish, and this was supposed to feed all these people! All the same, Andrew took the little boy to Jesus, and showed Jesus his packed lunch. To their surprise, Jesus told Andrew to make the people sit down, in groups of about fifty or so. Then he took the bread rolls, gave thanks to God for them and handed them to his friends to give to the people. Then he did the same with the two little fish.

And do you know, everyone got something to eat. Not just a few crumbs of food, but as much as they wanted, enough for them to be really full up. When everyone had finished, Jesus told his friends to collect up the food that was left – twelve whole baskets full of pieces of bread and fish! The people, and Jesus' friends were amazed at what had happened, and all because a little boy shared his packed lunch with Jesus.

Reflection

I'd like us to have a few moments now to think quietly about the story.

The little boy in the story was prepared to give away the little food that he had, even though it may have meant that he would go hungry himself. In the story, Jesus made the little boy's lunch feed all those hungry people. People who are Christians believe that God can do amazing things. They believe that God wants them to give him the little that they do have, so that he can turn it into a lot more.

Now there are many more things that we can share with each other besides food – we can share friendship, love and time with our families and friends. We may think that we only have a little to offer other people, but so did the little boy – and look what happened!

Prayer

Dear God,
The story we have heard told us about an amazing thing that Jesus did, all because a little boy was brave enough to offer him his small packed lunch. Help us to remember this when we feel we only have a very little to give.

Amen.

Suggestions for music

'Largo' from *Concerto in D for Lute and Strings* by Antonio Vivaldi

'Now Jesus one day' by Sister Oswin and Sister Margaret of Sion (to sing)

The servant who wouldn't forgive

Introduction

Forgiveness is a hard concept to explain, and even harder to live out! This assembly is a retelling of the parable of The Unforgiving Servant, told by Jesus in answer to a question about forgiveness asked by one of his disciples. It needs very little preparation.

Resources

- card
- string
- a crown made to fit you, if you're feeling brave!

Timing

15 minutes

Preparation

You will need to make two card labels to hang round children's necks. On one, write in large letters IOU £1 million; on the other write IOU £1. Then attach strings long enough to hang each label on a child.

Select two children from your class to wear these labels. They each have some very simple lines to learn.

Servant 1   Be patient with me. I will pay back everything (*and*)
            Pay me what you owe me!
Servant 2   Be patient with me and I will pay you back.

It needs only a little practice, and you will be giving them their cue in the story. It would be quite effective if they were to act as well, but it's not essential!

The Assembly

(Welcome the children and explain that this assembly is about forgiveness. Then continue by introducing the story.)

This is a story that Jesus told to one of his special friends. Peter had asked him, 'How many times must I forgive someone if they do something wrong?' So Jesus told him this story, to help him understand what it meant truly to forgive someone.

The story of the servant who wouldn't forgive

Once there lived a king (*Put on your crown.*) who decided one day that he must settle accounts with his servants. He called in the first servant (*The first child stands up.*) who owed him a great deal of money (*Hang the IOU £1 million label around the child's neck.*) – one million pounds! That's a lot of money!

But the first servant was not able to pay back what he owed. The king told him, 'Then you will need to sell all you own to pay what you owe me – everything you have must be sold.'

The first servant fell on his knees (*The first child kneels.*) before the king and said, 'Be patient with me. I will pay back everything.'

The king was a good and wise man, and he took pity on his servant. He told him, 'Because you begged me, I will let you off what you owe me – you now owe me nothing.'

The first servant went away, a much happier man. (*The first child stands again.*) But, unfortunately, that didn't last for long. He went and found one of his fellow servants (*The second child stands up.*) who owed him only a small amount of money. (*Hang the IOU £1 label around this child's neck.*) Only one pound – that's not very much!

He grabbed him and said, 'Pay me what you owe me!'

The second servant could not pay what he owed, so he fell to his knees (*The second child kneels.*) and said, 'Be patient with me and I will pay you back.'

But the first servant refused. Instead, he had the man thrown into prison until he could pay back what he owed (*The second child sits down.*). Imagine that – being sent to prison for owing just one pound! When the other servants of the king heard what had happened to their friend, they were very upset. They went to the king and told him all that had happened.

The king called the first servant back to him and said, 'You are a very wicked and cruel man! I let you off what you owed me because you begged me to. You should have shown the same mercy to your fellow servant, because I had shown you mercy by cancelling your debt.'

Angry and disappointed, he sent the first servant to prison for what he had done. (*The first child sits down.*)

At the end of the story, Jesus said, 'This is how God feels when you do not forgive people who have done wrong things.'

Reflection

Let us sit quietly and think about this story. The king we have heard about was angry and disappointed with his servant because he was so cruel to the man who owed him only one pound. Christians believe that God is disappointed when we don't forgive other people for the wrong things that they do to us.

All of us do and say things that are wrong. When we are hurt or upset by somebody else, may we be ready to forgive them, because we know that we have done wrong things sometimes, too.

Prayer

The prayer that I'm about to use is a small part of a famous prayer that Jesus taught to his special friends. Just listen to the words as I say them, and think about what they might mean.

Dear God
We are grateful that you forgive us when we have done things that we are truly sorry for.
Please help us to forgive other people when they do things that hurt or upset us.

Amen.

Suggestions for music

'Sorry' by Tracy Chapman

Use it, or lose it!

Introduction

This assembly is a retelling of The Parable of the Talents. It is very quick and easy to prepare. It could be used as one of a series on 'Stories Jesus Told', or even just as a warning of what can happen if we do not use what we have wisely. It can involve a whole class, with slightly more preparation, and presents an opportunity to act the story out, using a few simple props. It will also work just as well as a story in its own right.

Resources

- If you intend to use some children to act out the story, you need three children to be the servants. They must be able to follow instructions but need no rehearsing since you will be giving instructions as part of the story. You will also need:
- some artificial money (use classroom money, or make some)
- three card labels with string attached. The cards should have the following written on them:

  card 1 – 'servant 1' on one side and 'farmer' on the other

  card 2 – 'servant 2' on one side and 'fisherman' on the other

  card 3 – 'servant 3' only.

Timing

20 minutes

Preparation

Prepare the 'money' for the three servants – any amounts with a ratio 5 : 2 : 1. You could use £50, £20, £10, with 'home-made' £10 notes. You will also need enough 'money' to double the amounts given to servant 1 and servant 2.

If you want to involve the whole class, ask them to think hard about one thing that they are really good at – it might be reading, doing sums, skipping, doing up shoelaces, making up playground games. To set the children a real challenge, you could ask them to identify things that other children in the class are good at.

Choose a few children to prepare an example of what they are good at, to show the other children in the assembly.

If you do not want to use your class, then the question, 'What do you think you are good at?' could be asked of all the assembled children.

The Assembly

(Welcome the children and explain that today we are going to be thinking about our talents – what we are good at. Ask, 'What do you think you are good at?' or explain to the audience what some of the children from your own class are good at – and ask them to show what they have prepared. Then continue with the story.)

This is a story that is found in the Christian Bible. People used to come from all around to hear the stories that Jesus would tell. He told stories to help people to understand more about God and about how they should live their lives. People who are Christians believe that the stories Jesus told can still teach them how to live their lives today.

All of us are good at something, as those children were showing us just a few moments ago. Christians believe that everything that they have is like a present from God – their house, car, money, even themselves – and that this means that they should care for what they have properly. They also believe that God makes some people especially good at some things – they are talented in these things. Now you all know that all the things that you are good at need lots of practice – what would happen if you didn't practise? *(Allow a few children to explain – encourage them to say that they won't get better at e.g. reading if they don't practise.)*

Jesus told this story to make people think hard about what they should do with the things that God has given them.

The story of the talents

Once there lived a rich man who decided to go on holiday to a faraway country. He packed his suitcase and called his servants to him. He had three servants. *(Place labels around the necks of the three servants to show who is who.)* To the first servant he gave £50 *(Count out the money – get the children to join in with you.)* and said, 'Look after all I own until I return, and use this money wisely.'

To the second servant he gave £20 (*Count out the money.*) and said, 'Look after all I own until I return, and use this money wisely.'

To the third servant he gave £10 (*Count out the money.*) and said, 'Look after all I own until I return, and use this money wisely.'

Then off he went on his long holiday. The three servants thought long and hard about what they should do with their master's money.

The first servant thought to himself, 'I should like to make my master pleased with me,' so he went out and bought a small farm. (*Turn the label round to show 'farmer' and take the money from the servant.*) Because he worked hard, the business did well. By selling milk from the cows and goats, and eggs from the hens, he made twice as much. (*Ask if anyone knows how much that would be and count it out.*)

The second servant thought, 'I should like to make my master pleased with me,' so he went out and bought a small fishing boat. (*Turn the label round to show 'fisherman' and take the money from the servant.*) Because he worked hard, the business did well. By selling the fish that he caught, he made twice as much. (*Ask if anyone knows how much that would be and count it out.*)

The third servant didn't do so well. He was too lazy to use the money to buy anything, and was afraid he would lose what he had, so he hid the money where he thought no one would find it. (*Servant 3 hides the money.*)

After a long time, the rich man returned from his holiday and called his servants to him. He said to them, 'Go and bring me the money I gave you to look after.'

So the first servant gave him the money he had earned. The rich man was pleased and said, '£100! Well done, you good and faithful servant – you have used your money wisely. You have shown me you can take care of a little, so I will make you a ruler over many things. I am very pleased with you!'

Then the second servant gave him the money he had earned. The rich man was pleased and said, '£40! Well done, you good and faithful servant – you have used your money wisely. You have shown me you can take care of a little, so I will make you a ruler over many things. I am very pleased with you!'

Then the third servant gave him the money that he had kept hidden. To him the rich man said, 'You are a lazy and wicked servant. You could have at least put my money in the bank where it would have earnt me some interest. Give your money to my first servant so that he can use it more wisely than you did. Now leave my house and do not return!'

(The three servants can sit down to show the story has ended.)

Reflection

Let's sit quietly for a few moments now and think about the story we have just heard. The first two servants showed their master that they could be trusted, by working hard and using what they had been given wisely. The third servant wasted his chance by hiding the money and being lazy. Like the money that the servants were given, we all have things that belong to us and things that we are good at. We, too, need to be careful that we don't waste what we have, but instead use it wisely.

When we are tempted to be lazy, let us remember what happened to the lazy servant in the story – he was left with nothing. Let us try to be wise in all that we do and say.

Prayer

Dear God,
Thank you for all the things that we have. It is good to remember that we can all do something well. Help us not to be lazy, but be wise like the good servants, and use the things we have and the things we are good at well.

Amen.

Suggestions for music

Something quiet and reflective – such as 'Miss Clare Remembers' from *Watermark* by Enya

£10

£10

£10

Love is ...

Introduction

This assembly can be used either as a celebration of St Valentine's Day, or as part of a series thinking about feelings. It needs a little preparation in advance, but the work will be done mostly by your class. The assembly is based on a famous passage from the Bible, often read at wedding services, and aims to focus children on what Christians believe love is like.

Resources

- nine pieces of white paper cut into heart-shapes, for writing and drawing on
- red paper (if desired) to mount work.

Timing

20 minutes

Preparation

In advance, write the following statements, one on each of the nine pieces of white paper.

- When you love someone, you are patient with them.
- When you love someone, you are kind to them.
- When you love someone, you will be glad when good things happen to them.
- When you love someone, you will not boast when good things happen to you.
- When you love someone, you are not rude to them.
- When you love someone, you will not always want your own way.
- When you love someone, you will not be angry with them when they have done nothing to deserve it.
- When you love someone, you will forgive them when they do wrong things.
- When you love someone, you will be truthful with them.

(adapted from I Corinthians 13:4–6)

Explain to your class that you want them to think about what 'love' is for a few moments, then ask them to tell you what they were thinking about.

Now read the prepared statements to your class, explaining that they come from the Bible, which people who are Christians read to help them understand what God says about love. This part is often read to people in church when they are getting married.

Stop after you have read each statement and ask the children to tell you how they have been, or might be, patient or kind etc. with someone that they love.

At this point you will need to decide whether all your class will have some work to show, or just one child for each statement.

Ask each child who will be involved to draw a picture of themselves being patient, or kind etc. to help other children understand in the assembly. Mount their pictures on the red paper if desired.

The Assembly

Welcome the children and explain the theme for the assembly – and a little bit about St Valentine's Day if that is the reason for presenting an assembly on love.

Introduce the passage from the Bible, in much the same way as you did with your class. Then read out the statements, one at a time, and ask the child whose picture explains that statement to tell the assembled children what they are doing – if the children are a little nervous, you can help by asking them a question e.g. 'How are you being patient in this picture?'

Reflection

Loving someone is not always easy – there may be times for all of us when we don't feel like being patient or kind, or forgiving people when they do things that are wrong. People who are Christians often read those words that I read to you, to remind themselves of how they should behave towards people. Christians believe that God wants them to try to love people, even those who are not kind to them.

Let's have some quiet moments now while I read those words again – as I read, try to think about what they mean.

When you love someone, you are patient with them.

When you love someone, you are kind to them.

When you love someone, you will be glad when good things happen to them.

When you love someone, you will not boast when good things happen to you.

When you love someone, you are not rude to them.

When you love someone, you will not always want your own way.

When you love someone, you will not be angry with them when they have done nothing to deserve it.

When you love someone, you will forgive them when they do wrong things.

When you love someone, you will be truthful with them.

Prayer

Dear God,
You teach us that love is patient, love is kind, love is forgiving, never angry or jealous or rude. Help us to love in every moment.

Amen.

Suggestions for music

'Love is all around' (theme from the film *Four Weddings and a Funeral*) by Wet, Wet, Wet

'Love is the seventh wave' by Sting

Others first

Introduction

This was designed as a follow-up to the assembly 'Love is ...' (see page 122), although it is not vital that it should follow on. It is based on the Christian ideal of self-sacrifice – putting others first, a concept that is now quite alien in the 'me' culture in which we live today. It starts off with thinking about caring for each other as a way of putting the needs of others before those of ourselves, and then asks children to consider what Christians believe about self-sacrifice.

Timing

15–20 minutes

Preparation

A good way to prepare children for this assembly is to have a Caring day (or week if you prefer!) when you try really hard to care for each other. Discuss with your children how they could show they really care for each other, and add a few suggestions of your own if necessary.

When I did this activity with my own class, it was quite surprising how many of their suggestions were reinforcements of the good learning behaviour that we try consistently to instil in our children (such as not interrupting when someone else is speaking). I chose to reward any caring or kind act – no matter how small, since some children find it easier than others – with a sticker.

It is quite important for most of the ideas to come from the children – they have a greater sense of ownership over their behaviour if it has not been imposed on them.

Your class will need to be primed to explain their caring behaviour to others in assembly.

The Assembly _____

(Welcome the children and explain that the assembly is about thinking of other people before ourselves. Tell the assembled children about your class' Caring day – or week – and interview your children about the ways that they have been caring. Then continue.)

Having a Caring day (*or week*) was quite hard work for everyone. There were times when we all forgot to be kind, but the important thing was that we all tried so hard. When you look after someone, it makes them feel important. It makes them feel that you care enough about them to let them finish talking before you speak, or go first through a door, or take charge of a game when you would really like to be in charge.

The strange thing was that it made us happy too!

Christians believe that it is good to put others first. There is a verse in their special book, the Bible, which says, 'Put the needs of other people before your own needs' (*Romans 12:10, paraphrased*). That means that they will try to do whatever they can to help other people – whether they feel like it or not.

Jesus once said to his disciples, 'Love one another just as I have loved you.' (*John 15:13*). In the whole of his life, Jesus always put the needs of other people before his own needs.

This is a story from the Bible about putting others first. It tells of something that happened to Jesus and his friends as they were walking from a place called Galilee to somewhere called Jerusalem.

The story of the ten lepers

Jesus and his friends had just walked across the border from Galilee into a country called Samaria, when they noticed a small group of men walking a little distance away from them. At first, they thought that they were travellers like themselves. The men were moving very slowly, as if every step was painful to them, and as Jesus and his friends got nearer, they saw that these ten men had a dreadful disease called leprosy. Leprosy is an illness that affects the skin on people's hands, feet and faces.

In those days, people who had leprosy were sent away from their homes so that other people wouldn't catch the disease from them. Their only way of getting food was to beg for it, but they weren't allowed to go near people who didn't have the disease. So they had to carry a bell with them. They would ring this bell outside the villages, and some people would bring food to leave for them. There were no medicines to make their leprosy better, and so they would have to spend the rest of their lives alone.

When the lepers saw Jesus, they called out to him, 'Jesus! Master! Have pity on us.' Jesus' friends wondered what would happen next – surely Jesus wouldn't dare to go near these men, in case he caught the disease from them? But he walked towards them, and called them to come closer to him. Jesus' friends were amazed.

Jesus looked at the ten lepers and said, 'Go back to your village, and show yourselves to the priests.' The lepers looked surprised and explained to Jesus that they were not allowed to go near their village because of their disease. But Jesus told them to go, so they did.

And as they walked away, their leprosy started to disappear, so that by the time they reached their home, it had all gone. They were amazed! One of them, when he realized what was happening to him, rushed back to Jesus to say thank you, praising God all the way.

Jesus was glad to see him, but asked, 'Where are the other nine?' The man explained that they had all gone home to show their family and friends that they had been healed. Jesus was sad that only one man of the ten had bothered to come back to show how grateful he was, but said to the one man who had returned, 'Go. Your faith has made you well.'

Christians believe that they should try to be like Jesus in everything they do. For some Christians this means going to places that others wouldn't want to go to, or being with people who are very sick – just like Jesus did with the ten men who had leprosy. We may never feel able to do that, but there are many ways that we can show we care about other people.

As you go through today, there may be many chances for you to decide to put others first – it's up to you whether you take them.

Reflection

Let us be still for a moment and think about what we have just heard.

Do we put others first or are we selfish most of the time?

May we do our best to make other people happy – even when it means forgetting about what we want.

Prayer

Dear God,
As we go through today, please help us to put others first. Help us to do our best to make other people happy – even when it means forgetting about what we want.

Amen.

Suggestions for music

'When I needed a neighbour' by Sydney Carter (to sing)

Rules for living

Introduction

For children, part of school life is learning the rules that help the school to function effectively, and understanding why they are necessary. This assembly could follow the assembly 'Fun, but not fair!' (see page 10), which explored why it is necessary to have rules at all. This assembly starts from a place that is familiar to the children – school – and moves them on to consider the Ten Commandments given by God to Moses, and why they are important to Jews and Christians.

Resources

- paper – shaped like tablets of stone (The front of each tablet can be rubbed lightly with the side of a grey crayon to make it look more like stone – rubbing over the paper on a textured surface is quite effective.)
- a replica of the Torah (if you have one). These are available from mail order catalogues selling religious artefacts – see *Resources,* page 152.

Timing

20 minutes

Preparation

Ask your children to tell you some of the rules that you have as a class in your classroom, and any other school rules that they know. Make a note of what the children say – it may be necessary for you to make a few choices in order to keep your assembly to a manageable length. The assembly can involve your whole class if you have a lot of rules, or just a few children if you are aiming for something a little shorter!

Write these rules on one side of the 'stone tablets'. Then read the rules out to the children, one at a time, and ask them to consider what would happen if we did not have that rule, e.g. if the rule 'put your litter in the bin' was not observed, the playground would be full of litter and the school would look a mess. Some rules may need a little more discussion than others.

Ask the children to illustrate on the reverse of each 'stone tablet' what would happen if that rule was not obeyed.

The Assembly

(Welcome the children. If this assembly follows 'Fun, but not fair!', ask them if they can remember what the last assembly was all about. Then continue.)

We talked in the last assembly about why we need rules. (*Omit this reference if it is not appropriate.*) Today we are going to look at some of the rules that we try to keep in school – my class are going to help me here. We have been thinking about what might happen if everyone disobeyed – or didn't keep – the rules.

(Ask each child to read out their rule – or you read it if they are not able to – then explain their picture to everyone. After the last rule is shown, continue.)

All these rules are important to us because they make our school a safe and happy place to be in, and they help us to know how to behave towards people around us. The children's pictures showed what a mess we would be in if we didn't try to keep them!

In our assemblies, we often think about what different people believe. People who are Jews have ten special rules that they try hard to keep. They believe that God gave them the ten rules to help them to live good and happy lives. In their special book, the Torah (*Show them the copy if you have it.*), there is a story about God telling a man called Moses, one of the great Jewish leaders, to write down these rules on ten tablets of stone. (*If you have time, you could read some of the story here.*) The rules are:

1　Love God more than you love anyone else.
2　Love God more than you love anything else.
3　Do not swear.
4　Keep one day special when you can rest and worship God.
5　Love your mother and father and do as they say.
6　Do not kill anyone.
7　People who are married should love each other.
8　Do not steal.
9　Do not tell lies about anyone.
10　Do not want to have things that belong to anyone else – be happy with what you have.

Jewish people try hard all their lives to keep these rules because they love God and want to please him. They want to live good lives, but it isn't always easy, so when they pray to God, they might ask him to help them.

Reflection

It isn't always easy for us to keep the rules that we have in our life at school, and in our daily lives.

Let's have a few quiet moments now to think about the rules we have looked at in our assembly today – try to think of one that you find especially hard to keep.

In our lives, we have to try to keep many rules – at school and at home. It is not always easy to live by these rules, but we know that they are there to keep us safe and happy. Each day, may each one of us try harder to live by the rules.

Prayer

In this prayer, I shall be asking God to help us at the times when we find it hard. If you want to pray it with me, then you can join in with 'Amen' at the end.

Dear God,
In our lives, we have to try to keep many rules – at school and at home. We know that the rules are there to keep us safe and happy, but it is not always easy to obey them. When we find it hard, help us, we pray.

Amen.

Suggestions for music

'Give me joy in my heart', traditional (to sing)

Are you listening?

Introduction

This assembly needs little preparation, but will need a few props to help illustrate the introductory point. You need six children who are able to read simple sentences (either from your own class or chosen from the children in the assembly hall).The assembly is a retelling of a famous Hindu and Buddhist story, told originally to illustrate the nature of truth – here it is somewhat simplified to make it easier for children to understand. It focuses on the need to listen carefully to each other in order to learn important things, and to understand fully what truth is, as the story goes.

Resources

- an object with an interesting shape
- a 'feelie' bag
- six pieces of card.

Timing

15 minutes — including 5 minutes for the game

Preparation

Choose an interesting object – anything would do. The only criterion is that children should be able to touch different parts of it and not get too much of a clue what it is. The whole point of the exercise is that they try to build up a mental picture for the other children in the hall as to what they think the object in your bag is.

Put it in a large 'feelie' bag, so that it can be moved around by you fairly easily.

Write a different one of the following sentences on each of the cards:

Adviser 1: I think it's a snake.
Adviser 2: I think it's a spear.
Adviser 3: I think it's a fan.
Adviser 4: I think it's a wall.
Adviser 5: I think it's a rope.
Adviser 6: I think it's a tree trunk.

The Assembly _____

(Welcome the children and tell them that the assembly today is all about listening to each other.

You will need some volunteers to play a little game involving the 'feelie' bag. Each child must find only one part of the object in your bag and describe what the object feels like.

Remind the children in the assembly that they will need to listen carefully because you will be asking them, not the children who have felt in your bag, to guess what the object is.

You will need to play quite a large part in ensuring that they follow your instructions – move the object around so that each child stands a fair chance of feeling a different part. Several children will need to have turns, and they may need you to ask leading questions to help them describe more accurately. To make it fair, you could limit each child to a certain number of seconds for their turn.

Stop after a few minutes and ask the assembled children if anyone can guess what your object is. Remind them of what some of the children described – whether they are successful or not is unimportant, because the game is an exercise in listening to each other. But do show them what the object is if they don't guess – and congratulate them for trying, especially if they do guess correctly.

Next, explain, if you have not already primed six of your class, that you will need six children who are able to read quite confidently and who will listen for their place in the story that you are going to read. Tell them that it is only one sentence, and give the children you have chosen a few minutes to read their card to themselves. Arrange the children in order so that it is obvious who will come next.)

The story that I'm going to read to you today is all about listening to each other – or rather, what happens if we don't! The story takes place in India, and is often told to show people that it is wise to listen to each other.

The story of the six foolish men

Once there lived a king who had six advisers. Their job was to tell the king what to do when he had a problem to solve, and they were very proud that they had been chosen for this very important job. Each of the six men thought that he was the wisest and most important of all the king's advisers, and they would waste a lot of time arguing about it.

So one day, when the king was getting really fed up with listening to their arguments, he decided that he would give his advisers a test to see how wise they really were. He summoned his advisers to the palace and explained that he had a puzzle for them to solve. One by one, he blindfolded them, and took them outside and told them the puzzle.

'Here in front of you, is something that I want you to feel, and describe what it is like. Then, when you've all had your turn, you must tell me what you think it is.' And he led each blindfolded man, one at a time, to feel the object in front of them.

The first man (*The first child stands up.*) explained that he had felt something long and scaly that moved from side to side.

But the second man (*The second child stands up.*) disagreed. He explained that he had felt something that was smooth, hard and pointed at one end.

Now it was the turn of the third man (*The third child stands up.*) who had another idea altogether. He explained that he had felt something that was large and flat, and when he had touched it, it flapped in the breeze.

The fourth man (*The fourth child stands up.*) explained that he had to stretch his arms really wide to feel the object – it was tall, too, and felt solid.

The fifth man (*The fifth child stands up.*) had his turn next. He explained that he had felt something that was straight and thin, and had what felt like a stringy bit at the end.

Last of all, the sixth man (*The sixth child stands up.*) had his turn. He explained that he felt something that was large, and round, and solid, and went down to the ground.

When they had all had their turn, the king asked them to tell him what they thought the object was.

The first man said, (*Prompt child to read.*) 'I think it's a snake.' And he was pleased with himself, because he thought he had the right answer.

The second man said, (*Prompt child to read.*) 'I think it's a spear.' And he was pleased with himself, because he thought he had the right answer.

The third man said, (*Prompt child to read.*) 'I think it's a fan.' And he was pleased with himself, because he thought he had the right answer.

The fourth man said, (*Prompt child to read.*) 'I think it's a wall.' And he was pleased with himself, because he thought he had the right answer.

The fifth man said, (*Prompt child to read.*) 'I think it's a rope.' And he was pleased with himself, because he thought he had the right answer.

The sixth man said, (*Prompt child to read.*) 'I think it's a tree trunk.' And he was pleased with himself, because he thought he had the right answer.

When they had all given the king their opinions, he was amazed – not by how clever they were, but at their foolishness. Then the king took off their blindfolds so that they could see whether they had guessed correctly. They were amazed at what they saw. Each man had been so convinced that he was right, and that the others were wrong, that they had never even imagined that they were all feeling the same object.

There, in front of their very eyes was ... an elephant!

'You are very foolish men,' the king told them. 'Each of you was so convinced that you were right and all the others were wrong, that you never bothered to listen to each other. If only you had, you might have worked out that my mystery object was an elephant. Now I shall have to find some truly wise men who will take the time to listen to each other.'

Can you guess which part of the elephant each of the men was feeling?

The long scaly bit that felt like a snake?	the trunk
The smooth, hard, pointed bit that felt like a spear?	a tusk
The large, flat, flappy bit that felt like a fan?	an ear
The wide, tall and solid bit that felt like a wall?	the elephant's side
The straight, thin and stringy bit that felt like a rope?	the tail
The large, round and solid bit that felt like a tree trunk?	one of the elephant's legs

Reflection

Let us sit still for a moment and think a little about the story we have just heard.

All of the king's advisers were right in their own way – they had described very well what the object had felt like to them. But each man in the story was so busy thinking that he was right that he never considered that they could all help each other find the answer to the king's problem – they were too proud and too stubborn. They were all too keen to tell the king what they thought, but not very keen to listen.

For each of us, there will be times in our lives when we need to learn to listen to what someone else has to say before we make up our minds about something.

The story reminds us that it is wise to listen first and speak afterwards. Wherever we go and whatever we do, may we always be willing to listen to each other.

Prayer

Dear God,
The story reminds us that it is wise to listen first and speak afterwards.
Wherever we go, and whatever we do,
help us to be willing to listen to each other.

Amen.

Suggestions for music

Some Indian music – 'Govinda' by Kula Shaker or Ravi Shankar (sitar music)

Always doing good

Introduction

This is an Islamic story about something that happened to the Prophet Muhammad. It reveals how important it is to a Muslim always to do good, even when people do things to provoke you. It goes beyond the act of merely tolerating the acts of others – something that we as teachers are always trying to advocate – and actually going out of your way to be kind to them. This assembly is a very simple one to deliver, and needs hardly any preparation.

Timing

10–15 minutes

Preparation

The introduction to the assembly is a quick game of 'Consequences' – this is a rather more serious version though!

You will need to think up a few scenarios that will be familiar to the children – no doubt they will be all-too-familiar to you, having witnessed them first-hand on playground duty days! – such as:

- You are in the playground. You see a child who wants to play a game with their friends, but they say, 'No you can't. Go away!' What happens next?
- It is playtime. You see someone playing with their friend, when someone else comes along and pushes one of the children over on purpose. What happens next?

The scenarios are best kept impersonal, otherwise children will give the answers that they think they should give rather than what you, from experience, have actually seen happen!

The Assembly

(Welcome the children and tell them that you have a little game to play with them to help explain what you are going to be talking about in the assembly today. Reassure them that all they need to do is listen and then answer a question.

Encourage a few different responses to each scenario – there is no 'right' answer to each question; you are just asking them to report what they have seen happen. Then continue.)

All of us see things happen every day that make us sad – it is so easy to say or do something unkind back to the person who has been unkind to you. The story that we are going to hear today is about the Prophet Muhammad. He is called a prophet because he listened to Allah (*which is the Muslim name for God*) and told people what Allah said. This story is important to Muslims because it shows them how they should behave towards people who say or do unkind things.

The story of the woman who swept dust

The Prophet Muhammad travelled a lot from town to town, telling everyone about what Allah had revealed to him. Some people would stop to listen, but others would tell him they had no interest in what he was saying because they didn't believe that Allah had really spoken to Muhammad.

This story takes place in a little town near where Muhammad was living at that time. Each day, he would walk into the town and teach the people about Allah, and each day he passed the same woman, sweeping the dust from her house into the road.

One day, he stopped to speak to her, but she didn't want to listen to him. 'I've heard all about you and the lies you're telling people. Leave me alone!' she said, and she swept the dust from her house into Muhammad's path.

Every day Muhammad stopped to say some kind words to the woman, but every day she would sweep the dust from her house right into his path. And every time, Muhammad would smile and wish her well with the words: 'Peace be upon you.'

Then one day, when Muhammad came to her house, he noticed that she wasn't sweeping the dust as she usually did, so he asked the person who lived nearest to her where she was. The neighbour replied that the woman was not well.

Some of you might think that it served her right that she was not well after all the unkind things she had said and done to Muhammad. But not Muhammad. He went to the woman's house and looked after her until she was completely well again.

The woman was so moved by Muhammad's kindness to her, even when she had been so rude and unkind to him, that she became a Muslim.

Reflection

In the story, Muhammad repaid the unkind things that the woman said and did to him with only kindness. When she needed someone to look after her, Muhammad was there. Muslims believe that people should be kind to each other, no matter what.

When people hurt us or say things that upset us, we have to choose how to behave. We could do or say something that would hurt them back. We could choose to ignore them. Or, we could choose to do or say something kind, which would really surprise them and might make them ashamed of what they had just done to us. It is for us to choose.

Just think for a few quiet moments now – what will you do next time?

Prayer

Dear God,
Every day of our lives, each of us will have to make choices about how we will treat other people.
Help us to make the right choice – always to do good where we can.

Amen.

Suggestions for music

'I'll be there for you' by The Rembrandts

The thirsty camel

Introduction

Caring for animals is a very easy way into the whole area of looking after our world. The story that is used with this assembly is an Islamic one about the Prophet Muhammad, and deals with a Muslim's belief that we have a responsibility as human beings to care for all living creatures, because they are Allah's creation.

Timing

10–15 minutes

The Assembly

(Welcome the children to the assembly and explain that you are going to be asking them to think today about caring for all living things, and why this is important. Begin by asking the children these questions and getting a variety of responses.)

How many of you have a pet at home?

Who has a cat/dog/rabbit/hamster? *(Include as many animals as you wish to find out about.)*

What are the things that you have to do to take care of your pet?

What would happen if you didn't do them?

(After the discussion, continue.)

This is a story about a person who is special to people who are Muslims – the Prophet Muhammad. It tells of something that happened to the Prophet Muhammad one day, and helps Muslims to understand why it is important to care for all living creatures.

The story of the thirsty camel

In a place called Madinah, there were lots and lots of beautiful gardens – gardens as far as the eye could see, filled with exquisite flowers and tall trees. One day the Prophet Muhammad was walking through these gardens, enjoying the beautiful views. Lots of other people were there too, many of them sitting in the shade of the tall trees, or in the cooler parts of the garden, for the sun was hot and very strong. As he walked through the garden, Muhammad spotted two things in particular. One was a man, resting stretched out in the shade of the largest tree in the garden, obviously glad to be out of the glare of the sun. The other thing he noticed was a camel, tied up to a post in the hottest corner of the garden. It was howling because of the heat, so Muhammad went over to see what he could do. Not only was the poor camel very distressed and exhausted by the heat, but it looked thin, and its coat was in a very bad condition. The Prophet Muhammad stroked the camel and smoothed its poor, neglected coat, and the camel began to calm down a little. Then Muhammad spoke.

'Who does this camel belong to?' he asked in a loud voice, so that all the people nearby could hear. To his surprise, the reply came from the man he had noticed lying in the largest patch of shade. 'It's mine!' he said in a very cross voice, obviously annoyed that his afternoon nap had been disturbed.

'You should be really ashamed of yourself!' Muhammad said. 'This poor animal was entrusted to you by Allah (*which is the Muslim name for God*), so that it could help you by carrying you and all your belongings from place to place. In return you should care for its needs and make sure that it is well looked after, because it is one of Allah's living creatures. How dare you lie in the shade when your camel is in agony because it has no shade and no water!'

The story doesn't tell us what that man did about his camel, but I expect that you know what he should have done, don't you? I'm sure that you would be able to do a better job of looking after your pets than that man did of looking after his camel.

We may not have a camel to look after, but each of us knows enough about animals to know how to care for them, whether they are our pets or not. Muslims believe that it is important to care for every living creature, no matter how big or small, because, as Muhammad said in the story, they are 'Allah's living creatures'.

Reflection

Let's have a few moments of quiet now when you can think about the story that you have heard, and all the things that we have talked about today.

We are glad that our world is full of beautiful creatures, of all different shapes and sizes. May we do all that we can to show that we care for the creatures that we might see today. If we have pets of our own, may we give them all that they need to live happy, healthy lives.

Prayer

Dear God,

Thank you for all the wonderful creatures that are a part of our world. Please help us to do all that we can to show that we care for the creatures that we might see today. If we have pets of our own, help us to do all that we can to ensure that they live happy, healthy lives.

Amen.

Suggestions for music

'Lorenzo' by Phil Collins

'Washing of the water' from *US* by Peter Gabriel

Effective strategies

The following strategies for effective assemblies have been used in this book. They can be easily adapted for use with other materials, such as your own favourite stories.

Interactive assemblies

Another effective strategy is to take a theme and develop it over a period of four to six weeks. Here is an example using an interactive display. You will need to make a display or frieze in an area which is visible from any part of the hall or classroom. This could be a winter scene as illustrated on page 146. Cut out – or get the children to make – flowers, blossom etc. which can be stuck onto the display.

The introduction to this assembly will take about ten minutes, based on the following.

Talk about the scene depicted on the display board. Isn't it cold and dull? How can we make it more lively and interesting? Invite the children to help you turn this winter scene into spring. Tell them that every time they care for someone or something, including the environment, they can stick some cut-out paper flowers, grass, blossom, leaves etc. on to the display. Choose someone you have seen caring for somebody and invite them to stick on the first flower. As they do this, talk about what they did and how this made the other person feel. Tell the children that this display will be up for half a term (a lifetime!) and that we shall look at it during the next few assemblies. Tell the rest of the staff that they can send children out of the class to add to the display over the next few weeks, when they do an act of kindness.

At the end of the period, hopefully, you will have a wonderful spring display and a ready-made assembly, based on the following points.

- Do you remember what the display looked like a few weeks ago?
- Can anyone describe it?
- Isn't it beautiful now?
- Winter has turned to spring.
- Look at all these acts of kindness.
- When we care for someone, it makes them happy. Have you noticed that it makes you happy too, if you care for someone or something?
- Sometimes when we are alone or sad, we feel a bit like the wintry tree. When someone plays with us or helps us, it can make us feel like spring, full of life and colour.

The topic of spring could easily be replaced by other themes with linked displays, as follows.

Theme	Display
Christmas/Epiphany	• a present wrapped in dull paper becomes a multicoloured parcel
	• a dull Christmas tree becomes beautifully decorated
	• an interactive advent calendar
Ocean scene	an empty and lifeless ocean scene becomes vibrant: full of colourful fish and plants

and so on.

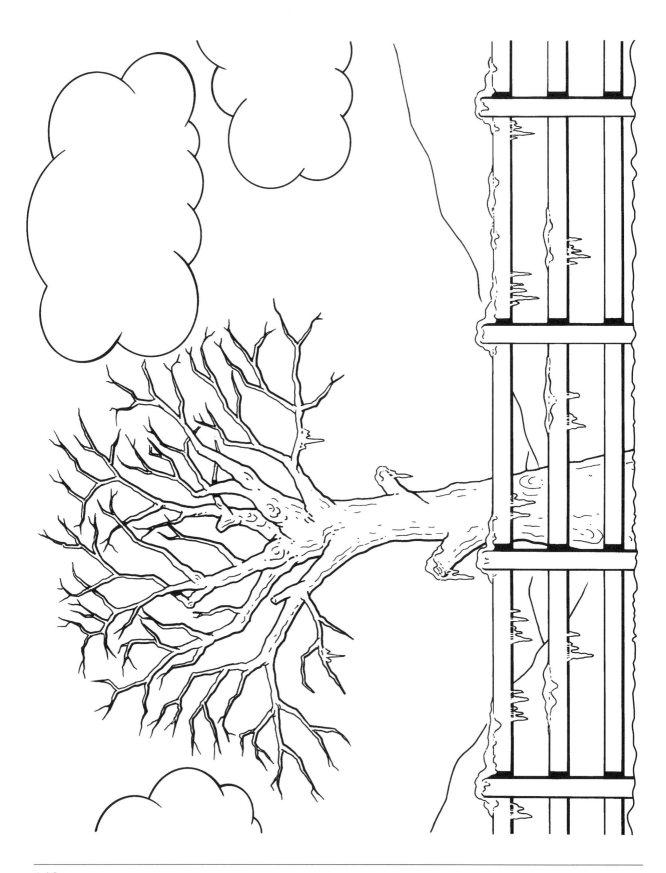

Two-year rolling programme

Planning your assemblies _____

Do you plan your assemblies well ahead, or are they the fruit of soul-searching the night before the event? Although the thought of planning one to two years in advance might seem like a nightmare, it can ultimately remove a great deal of heartache. The following table is an example of what a two-year rolling programme might look like. It is not intended to be comprehensive or the ultimate plan, but hopefully, demonstrates the benefit of planning ahead, especially if visitors are involved. It can also be made to dovetail with the rest of the curriculum.

We have given each half-term an overall theme which is based on a fairly typical spread of themes currently found in may infant schools throughout the country. We have chosen a two-year programme, as this is both manageable and neatly covers Years 1–2 at Key Stage 1.

We have then broken up each main theme into six weeks, which will, in turn, need to be broken down into daily assemblies. We imagine that two out of five of these days will be devoted to a music practice and the other will be a birthday or celebration assembly. (To ensure that these two meet legal requirements, it is advisable to include a moment of reflection.)

Those marked with an asterisk (*) are in this book, so this leaves you with plenty of opportunity for your own creativity and resourcefulness. You will want to add your own favourite assemblies. You may also want to recreate some of your favourite stories, using the strategies illustrated on pages 143–4 of this book. The suggested six-week themes could also be organized into three-week units if preferred.

Rolling Programme for Assemblies   Year A

Autumn	Spring	Summer
Main theme: **Our school**	Main theme: **Caring for our planet**	Main Theme: **We are special: talents**
1 Why are we here?* page 4	1 Waste not, want not!* page 99	1 We are all special* page 106
2 Working and playing together	2 Water of life* page 103	2 Beautiful inside* page 41
3 Fun, but not fair!* page 10	3 Save our world!* page 95	3 Are you listening?* page 132
4 Rules for living* page 129	4 Animals in danger	4 Talents in our school
5 New beginnings* page 52	5 The thirsty camel* page 140	5 Visitors with talents
6 Celebrations	6 Recycling	6 Use it or lose it!* page 117
Main theme: **Caring for others**	Main theme: **Brave people**	Main theme: **Special books 1**
1 Remember* page 61	1 If at first you don't succeed ...* page 17	1 Every little helps!* page 111
2 Building walls* page 20	2 Who's your hero?* page 81	2 Stories from the Old Testament
3 Sticky fingers* page 14	3 Bravery (St George)* page 84	3 Stories from the New Testament
4 Wish upon a star* page 67	4 Brave people in the Old Testament	4 Letters to God* page 38
5 Christmas	5 Brave people in the New Testament	5 Stories from many cultures
6 Christmas/Epiphany	6 Brave people today	6 Modern stories with a message

Rolling Programme for Assemblies   Year **B**

Autumn	Spring	Summer
Main Theme: Journeys / Main theme: **Being a friend**	Main theme: **Special books 2** / Main theme: **Feelings**	Main theme: **People who care for us** / Main theme: **Wonderful Earth**

Main theme: **Being a friend**

1 Co-operation* page 22
2 Promises* page 27
3 Watch what you say!* page 33
4 The hardest word* page 45
5 Forgiveness* page 36
6 The servant who wouldn't forgive* page 114

Main Theme: **Journeys**

1 *Sukkot** page 56
2 Journeys in the Old Testament
3 Journeys in the New Testament
4 *Hanukkah** page 64
5 Christmas presents* page 71
6 Christmas around the world

Main theme: **Feelings**

1 How to mend a broken heart* page 7
2 Take time to care* pages 144–6
3 Just around the corner!* page 88
4 Feeling new
5 Feeling happy sad, angry, lonely etc.
6 Coping with feelings

Main theme: **Special books 2**

1 Getting ready* page 74
2 Desert island discs* page 30
3 Special Books from different faiths
4 Easter Egg-stravaganza!* page 77
5 Bible Stories (Old Testament)
6 Bible Stories (New Testament)

Main theme: **Wonderful Earth**

1 Creation. Wonderful Earth
2 The days of creation (part 1)
3 The days of creation (part 2)
4 All things bright and beautiful
5 Creation stories from around the world
6 All the same, but different* page 91

Main theme: **People who care for us**

1 Love is...* page 122
2 Others first* page 125
3 Always doing good* page 137
4 People in our school who help us
5 Visitors to our school who help us
6 Showing thanks to those who care

Resources and useful addresses

SHAP Calendar of Religious Festivals

This authoritative calendar is published annually and is available at low cost (current price £3.50) from The National Society's RE Centre, 36 Causton Street, London SW1P 4AU. The information is accurate and annually updated, giving most of the major festivals for Christianity, the other World Faiths and more. The Calendar is accompanied by useful notes describing each festival. Telephone 0171 932 1194 and ask to be put on their mailing list.

Assembly file

This appears as a regular insert to *RE Today*. Published by CEM. This is one of the best RE and Collective Worship resources available. It is published termly and is full of excellent ideas for schools. Write to Christian Education Movement, Royal Buildings, Victoria Street, Derby DE1 1GW or telephone 01332 296655 and ask for the Primary mailing subscription. Price approximately £27.00 per year.

BBC Assembly materials

Assembly Kit, Primary Collective Worship
A collection of 20 short video clips spanning Key Stages 1–2. These are open-ended, thought provoking and most could be applied to Key Stage 1. Teacher's notes are included. Price approximately £30.00.

Something to think about (audio tape/CD)
This is designed specifically for five to seven-year-olds. If you are unable to tape programmes directly off the radio, tapes and CDs are available for purchase. Price approximately £8.00. There is also a teacher's resource book priced at £10.50.

Also available are audio cassettes and CDs of the music 'Come and Praise, Beginning' which accompanies 'Something to think about'. For further details of BBC resources for Key Stage 1 collective worship, write to:

BBC Educational Publishing, PO Box 234, Wetherby, West Yorkshire LS23 7EH.

The Practical Assembly Guide

Ann Lovelace, published by Heinemann, ISBN 0–435–302–40–X, price £24.95.

Although the assemblies are more for top of Key Stage 2 to Key Stage 4, the ideas and strategies used can easily be adapted for use with Key Stage 1. At £24.95 this may be too expensive to purchase for infant schools, but if you are part of a primary school, you might like to recommend it to your Key Stage 2 colleagues and then borrow it!

Tell me a story

Maurice Lynch, published by BFSS National RE Centre, Brunel University College, Osterley Campus, Borough Road TW7 5DU, telephone 0181 568 8741, ISBN 1–872–012–13–2, price £6.00.

An extremely useful bibliography for children's fiction which could be used for both RE and Collective Worship at Key Stage 1.

Moments and Messages (Choosing and using music for assembly)

Leonora Davies and Jenny Rose, published by BFSS National RE Centre (address above), ISBN 1–872012–15–9, price £3.50.

A useful document exploring the use of music in assemblies. Especially useful for ideas and sources for multicultural music.

Tapestry of Tales

Sandra Palmer and Elizabeth Breuilly, published by Collins Educational, ISBN 0–00–312000–7, price £12.65.

An excellent anthology of tales which can be easily adapted for use at Key Stage 1. The selection of stories from different faiths is particularly useful.

Red Letter Days

Jeanne Jackson, published by Stanley Thornes, ISBN 0–7487–1934–2, price £14.50.

A Key Stage 2 anthology, but informative about Christian saints.

The Lion Story-Teller's Bible

Published by Lion, ISBN: 0–7459–2921–4, price £9.99.

A book which has been highly acclaimed for classroom use in RE. The author manages to bring Bible stories alive for young listeners.

Nature's Trilogy (video)

Published by Readers Digest, Pegasus House, Blagrove, Swindon, SN17 6XX, price £39.99 for all three videos.

A three-video pack with wildlife footage, accompanied by classical music. Excellent photography which captures the interest of young children. Can be a useful alternative to just playing music at the beginning and end of assemblies.

Religious artefacts

There are now a number of mail order catalogues supplying religious artefacts to schools. For example: Religion in Evidence. Ring Freephone 0800 318686 and ask for their free catalogue.